THE FORMULA

Transform Your Dreams Into Reality

WHAT OTHERS ARE SAYING

"The step-by-step method employed in *The Formula: Turn Your Dreams into Reality* will make you realize that the only thing standing between you and achieving your dreams is *you*, and *you* are the person in charge of making things happen in your life."

Nancy Blitz,
Director of the Center for Teaching Effectiveness
and Professor of ESL at Arizona Western College

"This book is a must read for anyone interested in self improvement. Unlike most self-help texts, Dr. Barcomb gives the reader practical tools and techniques that *will* make dreams come true."

Stephen Shadle,
Attorney and Chairman of The First Bank, Yuma

"Since my husband is frequently on military deployment in hostile territory, *The Formula* has been a guide that has not only helped me cope but has changed my life in miraculous ways. I will also be referring to it daily to teach my two beautiful children how to become successful and happy adults and to do so in a fun and practical way."

Chrissy Clark,
Stay-at-home-mom and proud Army wife

THE FORMULA

Transform Your Dreams Into Reality

MARJORIE BARCOMB

Tate Publishing *&* Enterprises

Published by Tate Publishing & Enterprises, LLC
127 E. Trade Center Terrace | Mustang, Oklahoma 73064 USA
1.888.361.9473 | www.tatepublishing.com

Tate Publishing is committed to excellence in the publishing industry. The company reflects the philosophy established by the founders, based on Psalm 68:11,
"The Lord gave the word and great was the company of those who published it."

Book design copyright © 2010 by Tate Publishing, LLC. All rights reserved.
Cover design by Scott Parrish
Interior design by Lynly D. Grider

Published in the United States of America
ISBN: 978-1-61663-828-3
1. Self Help / Personal Growth / Success   2. Self-Help/General
10.06.28

DEDICATION

This book is dedicated to my family, and in loving memory of my mom, Lillian Therrien-Barcomb, who helped me learn the joy and the value of living by the universal standards of civility.

ACKNOWLEDGMENTS

I want to thank everyone who has been a positive influence in my life, and in helping me write this book. To my sons who have always encouraged me, I love you very much. My husband's patience is beyond measure; to him I extend my thanks and love. Mostly, I want to thank my Lord and Redeemer, Jesus Christ, who was my inspiration to write this book.

CONTENTS

Foreword — 13

Introduction — 15

Part I: How Do You Gain Confidence and Increase Your Chances for Happiness and Success? — **25**

Universal Standards Provide You with a
Solid Foundation upon which to Build Your Life — 27

Integrity Makes You Morally Whole — 37

Forgiveness and Reconciliation Set You Free — 53

Respect for Self, Others and the Environment
Provides for Teamwork and
Builds Strong Personal Relationships — 61

Responsibility Makes You Worthwhile — 95

Loyalty and Faithfulness Provide You Love and Security — 103

Service Provides Intrinsic Rewards and Increases
Your Self-Worth — 111

Fairness, Caring, and Thankfulness Earn You Respect — 117

A Decision-Making Model that Helps You Make
Defensible, Rational Decisions with a Clear Conscience — 123

Part 2: Who are You? — **131**

Who I am — 133

On the Surface, Who Do You Think You Are? — 141

How Have Your Life Experiences Affected You? — 151

Part 3: Who Do You Want to Be? — **157**

Building New Neural Pathways: Replacing Negative
or Destructive Thoughts and Habits with Positive
Constructive Ones — 159

Perseverance in the Face of Challenge Facilitates Your
Success — 171

**Part 4: How Do You get From Who You are
to Who You Want to Be?** — **175**

The Value of Writing Your Dream Statement and
of Setting Goals and Objectives — 177

The Strategic Plan for Writing Your Goals and Objectives,
Facing Challenges and Developing a Proactive Plan   187

Creating a Successful Feedback Loop   207

Appendix A   **213**

Action Verbs for Writing Objectives

Appendix B   **217**

Blank Goals and Objectives Worksheet

Appendix C   **219**

A List of Possible Self-Talk Statements

Endnotes   **229**

FOREWORD

I believe that nearly everyone, if asked, would indicate that they want to increase their chances for happiness and success in life. That is a reason many enroll in classes. It is why they pay for life coaches and counselors to help them build their confidence or attain their goals. It is why people buy self-help books like this one. Often, however, the courses and the coaches do not help as expected. The books do not deliver the promised strategies for success. I have some good news, however: This book *will* deliver its promise.

In the Self-Management class I teach at Northern Arizona University, I often have students review self-help books. My graduate psychology students are sophisticated in techniques of behavior change, and they provide good critiques. They recognize empty promises and faulty techniques. They did not find any of those in this manuscript. Instead, they found a refreshingly simple, clear, and well-presented series of steps that, if followed, are likely to help anyone fortunate enough to read the book move closer to achieving their dreams. Dr. Barcomb has concisely summarized a wealth of knowledge here acquired over her many years of successfully teaching character education courses. I've had the pleasure of working with her for over a decade, and I can attest to what a fine teacher she is. I am familiar with her high standards, her strong values, her wealth of knowledge, and her warmth and concern for all of her students. Now, I am very pleased to see that her teaching is no longer limited by the classroom walls, where it is a treasured well-kept secret, but is available to the world at large. If you follow the exercises Dr. Barcomb presents here in this engaging narrative, you will improve your own life tremendously. You will also improve the lives of those around you by the increased light you shine upon the world as a result of the new techniques and self-knowledge you acquire by reading this book.

Sherri N. McCarthy, Ph.D.
Professor of Educational Psychology,
Counseling and Human Relations
Northern Arizona University-Yuma
Fellow, Division 52, American
Psychological Association

INTRODUCTION

If you are ready to change or improve your life or to help others, you will find this book inviting and motivational. As a scientist, I find that the most beautiful scientific theories and laws are simple and practical. Using this simple approach, I have purposely steered clear of mind bending psychology jargon because "knowledge is a process of piling up facts; [but] wisdom lies in their simplification."[1]

It is my desire that you find this book easy to read and the techniques herein clear, practical, and easy to employ.

After dedicating decades to research and teaching with my focus on helping students to have a better life, I have found that there are five basic ingredients in finding success and happiness. They are:

1. Knowing, understanding, and incorporating timeless standards of civility which provide a basis for emotional and physical freedom from stress and negative consequences.

2. Doing self-examination to determine where your life has led you thus far.

3. Employing self-management techniques to get you to your desired destination with respect to your dreams and aspirations.

4. Preparing your dream statement (mission statement) and writing your objectives and goals using a formula that is simple, practical, and really works.

5. Creating a successful feedback loop by utilizing self-assessment, and monitoring and adjust-

ing activities through application of consistent, focused, and motivational strategies.

This book lays out the strategies that you can use as life-long, personal-development tools that you can quickly and easily learn to incorporate into daily living. This common-sense approach is intended for ordinary folks who really want to make a difference in their lives yet do not have knowledge of the psychology jargon that we find in most self-help or self-management books.

It is no longer enough to be smart—all the technological tools in the world add meaning and value only if they enhance our core values, the deepest part of our heart. Acquiring knowledge is no guarantee of practical, useful application. Wisdom implies a mature integration of appropriate knowledge, a seasoned ability to filter the inessential from the essential.[2]

A successful personal development regimen needs to be sensible, intentional, proactive, and a life-long process. Positive personal development does not happen by chance. If you wish to have a successful life there are things you must do to become a person who is committed to, has the courage to, and has the fortitude to do what is right in the face of political, family, and/or societal pressures.

Long-term success and happiness in fulfilling your dreams far outweigh the immediate pleasures of money, sex, drugs, and status. Living by a set of universal standards that have stood the test of time, and doing the right thing for the right reason are absolutely necessary to live a fulfilled life.

Freedom and wisdom are at the forefront of a full

and happy life. These two concepts should be understood, cherished, and defended if you plan to reach your personal, societal, and career goals. Both are necessary in eliminating stress and in making healthy choices.

FREEDOM

My mom used to say that in order to be truly free, you had to have a clear conscience; that is, you have to be a good and moral person. Also, she said that you had to be educated or trained so you could make career choices that would give you the freedom to live in the manner in which you chose. In life, even though I followed my mom's advice, I found that I wasn't truly free because I didn't forgive my dad for being so cruel to me as a child, and my career choice was simply to earn a living—not to fulfill a dream or passion. Now, I know that to be truly free you must have a clear conscience, an education, and/or training to pursue your dreams, as well as, your career choices, but most importantly the ability to forgive.

A CLEAR CONSCIENCE

As individuals develop their conscience, they learn that good feelings are associated with doing the right thing, and uncomfortable feelings are associated with doing the wrong thing.

Uncomfortable feelings such as worry and stress often trouble people who have not behaved in a way that was pleasing to their conscience. They become a slave to sleepless nights and develop a worrisome attitude—a dark cloud looms over them like a heavy weight, whereas, an individual with a clear conscience sees the light, smells the flowers and appreciates the morning dew. They sleep well and have a clear mind to attend to the things of the day. They do not fear being found out or being arrested or worse yet–incarcerated. They live a worry-free and wholesome life. They smile and let their light shine! I call it spreading "angel dust."

EDUCATION AND/OR TRAINING

Don't let anyone steal your dreams!! Thieves may steal your possessions, and a cunning person may steal your spouse, but no one can steal what you have developed and stored in your head. Even in death, no one can take your knowledge, your dreams, and your rational decision-making ability. These are personal possessions that are yours alone. Even when one's career doesn't seem related to his/her educational background, the ability to synthesize knowledge and to use rational logic can be put to use in any job. This ability provides freedom to make career choices and career changes. All learning is meaningful. Make sure you understand this.

FORGIVENESS

Forgiveness frees you from a very heavy burden. No one should carry such a burden. Bitterness is a by-product of the lack of forgiveness and negativity. It torments your mind and body. Bitterness and anger lead to many physical and mental ailments that destroy life itself, as well as the lives of others. A major spin off of bitterness is a life of crime. This can only be cured by true forgiveness. The development of a bitter attitude or the ability to forgive does not happen overnight. This is why intentional, proactive, life-long personal development is so crucial to living a successful and happy life. The life-saving, attitude development of forgiveness and thankfulness is an ongoing process that must be nurtured on a daily basis, and it is your job to persevere in this arena for a life-time.

Today we see much bitterness, anger, and hatred in our country and in the world. What has caused such bitterness and resentment? I think it's because we have allowed our media and society to desensitize and brainwash us into believing that we are not responsible for our actions. It seems that there is always someone else upon whom to place the blame. We see chronic finger pointing both in political life and in everyday life.

The focus has been taken off the problem solving aspects, and the convictions we should live by, both of which are critical components for the survival of a free society. It seems that the blame game has become the rule of the day. A prime example is that our prisons are full of people who still blame others for their actions and their incarceration.

Another example is that in the political arena, we generally hear nothing but lies and criticism, yet we see little or no ongoing substantive problem solving processes or the courage to live by and stand up for moral convictions that would provide alternative viable solutions. It's time for politicians to step up to the plate, stop blaming others, and take responsibility for their actions.

The blame game must end. If you want to be independent, free, and responsible; it is your duty to forgive and to understand the consequences of your actions. Forgiveness frees the spirit. It is in respecting ourselves, our health, and well-being that we forgive; not only that, it is simply the right thing to do.

Sometimes it is difficult to forgive. It takes moral courage and a strong, independent attitude to forgive; but no matter how hard we have to work at forgiving, the priceless reward is personal freedom from the bondage of bitterness and its destructive by-products.

In your personal development you should enjoy modeling forgiveness in your day-to-day affairs. When you forgive someone for wrongdoing, it does not mean that you condone the improper behavior, but you do forgive the person. In many cases you may be forgiving a family member, but you still love them. We have all done things in the past for which we need forgiveness and truly appreciate it when we are forgiven. Therefore, we too must forgive others.

There are times, however, that you must stand firm. Events occur that you should not tolerate. Sometimes you have to be courageous and fight for and even die for things you strongly believe in. For example, I would gladly give up my life to save one of my children. I would gladly give up my life to maintain the degree of freedom we enjoy in our wonderful country.

Even though you may encounter major dilemmas in life, overall, forgiveness is the ticket to happiness and prosperity. The joy and freedom resulting from forgiveness make forgiveness one of the most important attributes you can acquire in your lifetime and one that you must model for the benefit of others. It is a major component in determining the degree of success you can attain.

WISDOM

There have been many wise men and women throughout the years. Probably, one of the most notable, other than my mother, was King Solomon. Solomon prayed for wisdom, and as a result of his gift of wisdom, he is credited with over one thousand songs and three thousand wise sayings, many of which can be found in the books of Proverbs, Ecclesiastes, and Song of Songs. My favorites are found in Proverbs from Chapter 1 through Chapter 9. Here you will find instructions on wisdom and foolishness.

If you intend to live a fulfilled life, you owe it to yourself to seek wisdom and good advice for daily living. Today, more than ever, the pressure of *worldly* pleasures, by peers and the media, challenges us all, even if we have been raised with excellent family values. How frightening it is to think of living life without incorporating character-building as a life-long goal. Good character is a pre-requisite for all other successes that lead to true happiness.

Wisdom is the richest of all riches. The wealth garnered from wisdom is in knowledge and understanding. It is in walking in the sunshine with joy pouring from your heart. It is in happiness that comes from within rather than from worldly pleasures from without. Wisdom gives you the courage that takes you through tough times and tough decisions. Wisdom teaches you to learn to look back and ask, "What was I supposed to learn from that?" This process helps you grow in personal development as a result. As you grow in your personal development, success is sure to follow. The wise are not led astray.

The wise understand and ascribe to being thankful every day. Wisdom is medicine for curing depression and boredom. Even though you may be tested by illness, unemployment, abandonment, or other trials, by keeping your mind filled with thankfulness you will learn to rise above your circumstances and emerge stronger in the end. One who is not taught to give thanks on a daily basis can easily slip into depression and self-pity. Wisdom provides the basis for mental and spiritual health to keep that from happening.

FREEDOM AND WISDOM

Freedom and wisdom should always be at the forefront of all your thought processes. It is in being free and in being wise that you can muster up the army of neurons in your brain to go to work for you. They need to have a clear path. Lack of freedom and lack of wisdom clutter up these brain super-highways, and your job of attaining happiness and success and of fulfilling your dreams becomes a very burdensome chore.

THE BOOK CONTENTS

- Part 1 will give you the tools to know, feel, and act in concert with universal standards that energize your conscience and build your character.
- Through thoughtful self-evaluation, Part 2 will help you to understand who you are, and why you have become that person.

  MARJORIE BARCOMB

- Part 3 will give you the tools to become who you want to be.
- Given what you have learned in Parts 1–3, Part 4 will give you a strategy to use in planning for your happy and successful future. It will also show you a process that will help you stay on track as you continue your life-long learning quest of personal fulfillment and personal development.

PART I

HOW DO YOU GAIN CONFIDENCE AND INCREASE YOUR CHANCES FOR HAPPINESS AND SUCCESS?

UNIVERSAL STANDARDS PROVIDE YOU WITH A SOLID FOUNDATION UPON WHICH TO BUILD YOUR LIFE

"Nothing in life is to be feared.
It is only to be understood."[1]

"Every human being has…an attendant spirit; [a conscience], and wise are they who obey its signals. If it does not always tell us what to do, it always cautions us what not to do."[2]

People whom you respect and admire have charisma that generally results from being highly principled. They exude confidence and display a happy persona. These people know what they want, who they are, and are clear about it. They seem sure about themselves, and are confident about the direction in which they are headed. They guard their reputation and carefully select the words and topics of their conversations. They remain consistent through good times and hard times. What is of utmost importance is they seem happy with whom they are and in what they do.

Do you have a driving desire to become a highly principled person? "The habits of feeling, action and judgment that comprise good character depend on personal self-discipline and powerful aspiration to become a good person, all of which must be drawn from within."[3] When the going gets tough, when the chips are down, what do you do? What you do lies at the essence of your character. How you respond to your strengths and successes, weaknesses, and failures, and challenges and opportunities also are an indicator of your true character.

You will get to examine the indicators of what you would do in these situations; you will see who you really are on the inside, your true character. Will you like what you see? Do you think you may want to make some changes? What greater gift can you give yourself than to learn to become a highly principled person? Are you ready?

Many people want to build their lives–but without a strong foundation based on the universal standards of civility, it's like building a beautiful house with a weak foundation. It may look great for a while, but eventually it will crumble. The same is true of your dreams and aspirations. Unless your life is built on strong ethical principles or universal standards that have withstood the test of time, what you have built is subject to collapse. Those who work tirelessly on their goals and objectives but seem to run into difficulty every step of the way may have a weak or faulty foundation with respect to standards of civility we should live by. The cornerstone of human civilization rests on ethical and moral codes.

Thomas Lickona, author of *Educating for Character*, says that the three basic components of good character are moral knowing, moral feeling, and moral action.[4] Therefore, when you know, feel and act in concert with high principles, you gain confidence, and your whole life changes; you become happier and more successful. You are sought by others who want to become like you. By developing skills that lead you to know, understand, and act in a

　　　　　　　　　　　　MARJORIE BARCOMB

manner congruent with universal standards that have withstood the test of time, you learn to make rational decisions that you can defend in any situation. Believe it or not, there are universal standards that transcend all cultures, races, and religions.

Developing character-building skills is not a quick fix solution. Learning skills that build your character and ultimately your confidence and understanding of who you are as a person should be a life-long, personal-development endeavor. Being proactive can make an unbelievable difference in how fast this can happen. No matter how principled you may feel that you are, success and happiness comes from an honest self-evaluation and a life-long quest for learning self-management and self-improvement techniques.

It is very easy to make rational decisions when your thinking embodies a clear Decision Making Model that is based on timeless universal standards. When you make fair sound decisions, your confidence soars and good things seem to happen.

We don't have to be sick to get better. Personally, I review the character-building strategies frequently, and each time I do, I find something new to add to my life. I think of new ways to incorporate these standards into everything I do. This has helped me to build lasting relationships and to gain the respect of others in ways that I never dreamed possible.

Unfortunately, we live in an era of great corruption, deception, rebellion, and moral decay. Because of the lifestyle that many have chosen to follow, we see horrible consequences, such as murder, suicide, domestic violence, horrendous drug addiction, incarcerations, diseases, violent sex crimes, etc. What I find so sad is that many have chosen to follow disastrous paths but have not done so based on good clear thought. They too, are the victims of our greedy present day society. Those people may not be reading this book, but you are! And, you can make a difference by utilizing the tools described herein. By modeling what you have learned or by 'dripping' on others in your conversations, you can do great things. By becoming more proactive, each individual can do a lot to improve not only his or her life but that of the status quo. Wouldn't it be wonderful if the old hand-shake was as good as a witnessed and notarized contract? As an individual, you can make your word as good as that contract.

It's amazing how one small sentence or phrase of praise or encouragement can make all the difference in someone's life. I'm always overwhelmed when prior students approach me and say, "You changed my life" and go on to tell me what I said or did. Generally, I don't even remember the event, but by making sure you always stay positive and have a loving attitude, you do indeed change lives. "Be careful what you think. Your thoughts run your life."[5]

Crimes against children are rising at an unprecedented rate, major Ponzi schemes are responsible for serious jail times, and no one trusts the government any longer. Wow, what a serious testament to where our values or lack of values have taken us as a society! How can these corruptors have happiness? They cannot! Think of Bernie Madoff; was he really successful? Think of the consequences. Was it worth a 150 year jail sentence? Think about the many poli-

     MARJORIE BARCOMB

ticians who have ruined their family's lives and their careers for the immediate gratification resulting from fraudulent schemes or infidelity. The long-term consequences are devastating.

"The greatest obstacle to being a person of character and leading an ethical life is the dominance of self-centered, pleasure-seeking values—feeling good, satisfying passions and urges and avoiding pain and discomfort at all costs."[6]

If an opportunity sounds too good to be true, it probably is. If the cost–benefit ratio of an opportunity shows high gain and low risk, it probably is unethical. Don't surrender your principles for a fast buck. Have the moral courage to remain committed to the universal standards you will read about in subsequent chapters.

Sometimes we have to stand up for what is right, even though others may say that we are intolerant. As a society, we have become so afraid to speak up about right and wrong for fear of being called intolerant or not politically correct that we turn a blind eye and a deaf ear to the gross inappropriate behaviors of many, especially those in so-called high places. Just because someone is powerful or rich doesn't mean that they should have the right to live immoral and destructive lives. The worst part is that they become role models for us and our children. We have to be ever so vigilant and submerge ourselves and our families in the timeless standards of civility.

Many people become role models because of their talents. Singers, sports figures, actors, and other people in the lime-light become role models. These people are lucky that they have been endowed with these gifts. These gifts are freely given by their creator. These folks are not necessarily people of stellar character; in fact, many are just the opposite. It is unfortunate that many look up to them as though they were gods.

It is frustrating to see the success of many talented people who are drug addicts, rogues, and immoral in many ways. But we must always remember that in the end, it is our character that wins out. Don't ever give up on becoming a highly principled person; it will serve you well.

Conversely, good character is not a gift that is freely given; it is built brick by brick, step by step, and bit by bit through careful thought, hard work, and dedication until it becomes a solid rock upon which intelligent and fair decisions are made.

Some people think that being a good person means that you conform to the current social norms. What if the social norms do not conform to being a person that lives by the universal standards of civility? Do you go against the status quo, or do you just go along with the rest of the pack? Many followed Adolph Hitler because his beliefs had become the social norm. People of character did not follow the social norm and many lost their lives because of it. But I'd rather have my gravestone say that I died prematurely believing in freedom for all than to have lived longer and ultimately be remembered as the Butcher of Auschweitz. If everybody is doing it, it doesn't mean it is right. "If everyone was jumping off the bridge, would you jump, too?" Don't confuse cultural norms with universal standards of civility.

You may wonder why so many who steal, cheat and lie never seem to get caught—that crime does seem to pay.

                                    MARJORIE BARCOMB

Why should you traverse the straight narrow path? Why should you not stoop to the level of the unethical?

- First, it is your moral obligation to do the right thing and to do it for the right reasons. Whether you know it or not, you are a role model for someone.
- Second, your self-worth, your self-respect, and the respect you get from your family and those who are close to you are in jeopardy when you fail to exhibit high moral standards.
- Third, employers, co-workers, and your peers will seek your guidance and counsel and provide praise and approval when you consistently exhibit moral fortitude.
- Finally, happiness is not just praise, money, a promotion, or getting a high grade on an exam. Happiness comes from within, and if you are not happy with whom you are on the inside, you can never have total and complete happiness in your life.

"We teach by what we do, not by what we say."[7] People who are only interested in themselves and not the greater good are subject to immoral and/or unethical behavior and may for a time seem to succeed, but eventually they are found out. We cannot help the way many in society carry on their lives, but we should live our life the way life ought to be lived.

In this day and age, I realize that because of outside pressures and the human desires that are nurtured and exploited by our media and other outlets we must be guarded and truly committed to do what is right, no matter what. Be proud and cultivate the strength you have to control your life.

Because of our life-long programming, we have to take a serious look at what we do and who we have become and take the necessary steps to remain or get on a wholesome, confidence-building track for happiness and fulfillment. "Nothing about character is hereditary. Everyone, regardless of social background, financial status, race, or sex, enters the world with an equal opportunity to become a person of great or petty character."[8]

The value of good character was clearly evident in the results of a survey conducted by my students who were enrolled in an Alternative Education class at Northern Arizona University. My students and I worked cooperatively on a survey to determine what qualities local businesses were seeking in prospective employees. Each student was assigned to give the survey to ten businesses. We tabulated and analyzed the data. The results were significant. Most businesses were looking for employees with values, with the most important value being honesty. Not one of the businesses indicated that they were more interested in qualifications! Many applicants are well-qualified for the job, but their personality flaws and lack of values make them unsuitable, so they don't get hired. In most cases, people get hired because of their qualifications, but they get fired because of their personality flaws. Instead, wouldn't it be nice for the employer to say, "Well done, you upright, honorable, admirable, and faithful employee?" or "You are faithful, trustworthy, loyal, incorruptible, steady, and true."

I'm always astonished that schools spend so much time on teaching to the test so their students pass state exams, and totally ignore the most important aspects of human civility. Teddy Roosevelt had it right when he said, "To educate a man in mind and not in morals is to educate a menace to society."[9]

Our schools have changed their focus and mission from developing well-rounded students to focusing on academic, state-mandated proficiency exams. It is for this reason that I feel that the lack of universal values is becoming more and more prevalent in the younger generation. It is not their fault. Parents work, and the schools either ignore these timeless standards or fear the repercussions of teaching them. It is frightening!

Unfortunately, many adults, both young and old, lack the confidence that should rightfully be theirs because they lack knowledge, understanding, and love of universal standards. Without this, they do not have a strong personal conviction to these timeless essentials for civility, nor a basis for making fair and just decisions.

To quickly and easily incorporate these standards in all that you do, you must be willing to assign yourself simple daily practice. Your very nature learns through daily practice to embody universal standards that will assist you in making not only life-changing but life-enhancing decisions. Hopefully, you will be willing to share what you have learned with others.

There are many descriptors that can be used when listing basic universal standards, but for the purpose of clarity and simplicity, Part 1 will include the following over-arching standards that subsume all others:

- Integrity
- Forgiveness and Reconciliation
- Respect for Self, Others, and the Environment
- Responsibility
- Loyalty and Faithfulness
- Service
- Fairness, Caring, and Thankfulness

Each of these standards will be thoroughly discussed so that there are no gray areas. The test of reversibility is always a simple guide as to whether an action is right or wrong. For example, honesty is better than dishonesty. By applying these standards when making decisions, you have the basis for making a rational, defensible case that builds your confidence, and that is the first step in getting your life headed in the right direction. "The mind grows by what it feeds on."[10]

                                    MARJORIE BARCOMB

INTEGRITY MAKES YOU MORALLY WHOLE

*"Integrity requires both being true
to oneself and living up to one's
highest and best personal values."*[1]

Integrity can be best described as moral wholeness and the king of all other values. Webster describes integrity as:

1. An unimpaired condition; soundness
2. Firm adherence to a code of especially moral or artistic values; incorruptibility
3. The quality or state of being complete or undivided; completeness

Since integrity is the king of values, many other personal attributes fall under the umbrella of integrity or moral wholeness. The personal attributes that are fundamentals of the universal standard of integrity include the following: truthfulness, honesty, promise keeping, reliability, and trustworthiness.

TRUTHFULNESS

"I hope I shall always possess firmness and virtue enough to maintain what I consider the most enviable of all titles—the character of an honest man."[2]

You can tell the truth for a life-time, and then you tell one lie and get caught. What happens? You become known as a liar. Ouch! You have just toppled the tower of trust. To be an honest person you must speak the truth and make sure your actions match your words. Think before you speak to make sure you are sincere about what it is you have to say. Don't just tell people things that you think they want to hear! Be truthful or be silent. Guard your reputation and elevate your character by practicing honesty. Don't let yourself slide down the slippery slope of deception. One little white lie leads to another and then it gets easier and easier to lie further. Soon your love for the truth starts to disappear. Remember, whatever you practice becomes part of your programming. "Truth leads to virtue…A person continues to speak the truth until he becomes thoroughly truthful."[3]

Do you know someone who exaggerates or distorts the truth? What a great way to lose friends. How about excuses? I think excuses are lies; otherwise, they are not excuses but the true state of affairs. For example, someone is late and says they had a flat tire. If it's a lie, it's an excuse; and if it's the truth, it's actually what happened, and it's not an excuse. Mistakes happen, but don't use this as an excuse. An example of a mistake is when you accidentally write a lunch engagement in your calendar on the wrong day. You know the truth. And the truth is you know you made a mistake.

Have you ever had someone lie to you because they didn't want to hurt your feelings? Were you happy about that? Then put yourself in your friend's shoes and ask yourself if they found out that you lied because you didn't want to hurt them, would they be happy with your decision or

     MARJORIE BARCOMB

would they be disappointed with you? Your answer will determine what you should do.

Some people think that being sneaky, tricky, or deceptive, is not being dishonest; it is simply getting something over on someone else, and, unfortunately many enjoy doing it. Not only is this dishonest, it is deceitful. People who do this have the need to control. How sad, but they scream the loudest when the tables are turned. These people have not found happiness.

Hiding the truth is just another way of being dishonest. What will the person from whom you have hidden the truth say when they find out that you knew but hid the truth from them? When people find out you've lied or hidden the truth, they may be hurt or even explode. How do you feel when you have been lied to? The best rule to follow is the Golden Rule: Treat others as you would like to be treated.

"This above all: to thine own self be true/ and it must follow, as the night the day/Thou canst not then be false to any person."[4]

In his book, *What To Say When You Talk To Your Self,* Shad Helmstetter goes into great detail about self-talk.[5] This book is another very useful tool as you prepare to become the only person who can change your life. As I said before, my intention is to give you tools that are easy to understand, and to easy to apply to your life and self-talk is the first tool.

Practice your self-talk, create your mental imagery, and monitor your actions.

Every Day Say:

I am honest. I *am* honest. I am *honest*.

I always tell the truth. I *always* tell the truth. I always *tell* the truth. I always tell the *truth*.

Think of each word you are saying as you emphasize each important word in the saying. Say each of the above every day without missing a day for at least thirty consecutive days, and see what happens. Write the sayings on a 3X5 card and put the card where you will see it and read it over and over each day. Remember, if you miss a day, you have to start over again. This exercise is designed to assist in building new neural pathways to re-program your brain. This is called, The Rule of Thirty Days.[6]

Helmstetter spoke of The Rule of Thirty Days at a national conference I attended in 2006. He alluded to an experiment that was conducted by NASA, wherein they found that it took thirty days to create new neural pathways. The experiment dealt with wearing glasses that inverted images. After thirty days of wearing the glasses, the astronauts' brains had compensated by building new neural pathways, and they saw the images in their upright position even though they were still wearing the image-inverting glasses. The interesting off-shoot of this experiment was, if they took the glasses off any time before thirty days, they had to start all over again.

The affirmation through self-talk is done to pass a command from the conscious mind to the sub-conscious mind. Once your sub-conscious accepts what you have said as true, it will become a reality. If you kind of choke on some of the self-talk suggestions because you know full well that it is not true in your case, you can say the affirmation using, "I choose" in the statement. For example, suppose a smoker would find it difficult to say, "I do not smoke." He or she may find it much easier to say, "I choose not to smoke." Another requirement is your self-talk statements are in the present tense. "Great thoughts reduced to practice become great acts."[7]

The second tool deals with creating mental images or visioning situations where you see yourself as a highly principled person. In keeping with applying practical principles, I will not go into the cognitive psychology of mental imagery or visualization. I think common sense tells us all that we can in our mind's eye create a picture of any situation. It is my hope that these positive mental pictures provide the kind of positive affirmation, coupled with your self-talk, to make your life changes more rapidly and long-lasting. In the beginning, I will offer some images, but you will soon discover that you will become very adept at conjuring up your own images that fit your personality and your life's situation.

After completing your self-talk, create and practice your mental imagery. For example, picture yourself in a situation where you are telling the truth. It may be in a benign situation or it may be in a situation where you are uncomfortable telling the truth. Picture yourself mustering up the courage to tell the truth anyway. Picture your boss asking you about your friend's work performance that you know has been slipping lately. What do you say? You may have to work on your mental imagery in the beginning, but it is fun to picture yourself as the person you want to become.

The third and last part of your practice session asks you to monitor everything you say each day, and to evaluate yourself in the evening on how honest you were in all situations. Make sure to praise yourself for paying close attention to your words and ask yourself, "What can I do to improve, tomorrow?"

Whether you are doing self-talk, practicing imaging, or acting in concert with the universal standards, remember to apply the Rule of Thirty Days.

HONESTY

> "Whoever can be trusted with small things can also be trusted with large things; whoever is dishonest in little things will be dishonest in large things, too."[8]

We have all had something taken from us that made us sad, angry or upset. Even though what may have been stolen has little value to the thief, it may have great sentimental value to you. When you have been robbed, it hurts and leaves you feeling violated and vulnerable. On the other hand, no matter how honest people think they are most are a bit dishonest and don't even realize it. Again, our society is de-sensitized to a strict code of ethics.

I'm always surprised at the number of people who steal the little things: paper, pens, pencils, and other office supplies from their employer. And the worst part is that they think it is okay. Another great example of stealing that seems to be well tolerated by modern society is the copy-

MARJORIE BARCOMB

ing of copyrighted materials, especially computer software. People have worked hard to create computer software, and to steal it is just as criminal as walking into the office supply store and stealing the software off the shelf.

Many people think that they are being moral because they can always cite someone who has done worse. Our moral compass reading should not be based on what someone else does, but on what we have learned as moral principles that we should live by. Just because everybody is doing it doesn't mean it is right.

Cheating is another vice that seems to be the norm. When asking students how many have cheated on homework or exams, most say that they have. Why? Because everybody is doing it! This leads to cheating on taxes, cheating on your spouse, etc. Remember, your reputation is what people think you are, but your character is what you really are and only you know that. Do you like who you are right now? Can you improve?

It is vital that you must strive for continuous improvement but none of us will ever be perfect. We must work at improvement every day so that we can be joyful and secure. "The honest person will live safely…But dishonesty will hurt those who are not trustworthy."[9]

Practice your self-talk, practice your mental imagery, and monitor your actions.

Every Day Say:

- I am honest.
- I never take anything that isn't mine.

- I never copy copyrighted material, and I don't cheat.

Don't forget to stress each important word in the *saying* and keep in mind the Rule of Thirty Days which says if you miss a day you have to start over again. I wish I could hear your comments after thirty days!

Now practice your mental imagery. Picture yourself with a friend who is offering you to copy his disk that contains a program or game that you have been wanting for some time. Make sure you tell him that you are really working hard on becoming a highly principled person and that copying the disk wouldn't be fair to the person(s) who worked hard developing the program or game. Now, feel really good about what you have said. Just think, soon your friends will not be asking you to do things that are not in sync with the standards you have set for yourself. Who knows, what you say may even impact your friends in a positive way.

Finally, monitor everything you do each day, and evaluate yourself in the evening on how honest you were in all situations. Make sure to praise yourself for paying close attention to your actions and ask yourself, "What can I do to improve, tomorrow?"

PROMISE-KEEPING

"Losers make promises they often break. Winners make commitments they always keep."[10]

Keep your promises. We all have had someone promise us something, and then break their promise. We wait patiently

                    MARJORIE BARCOMB

yet anxiously for the fulfillment of the promise only to be hurt and let down. Again, the golden rule: Do unto others as you would have them do unto you.

I have found in my many years that people seem to find it okay to promise something to make others feel good at the time, yet have no intention of keeping their promise. "Commitment is doing the thing you said you'd do, long after the feeling you said it in has passed."[11] That is keeping your word!

This reminds me of a friend who bought some property and built a camp in Alaska. Many friends promised Marilyn that they would go to Alaska when she invited them. They did not go, and had no intention of going! When I pondered that I too had promised to visit her in Alaska, I decided to re-evaluate my commitment to her. I immediately went to the phone and asked her when it would be convenient for my visit. I got the plane tickets and made the trip. I must say that the visit and the salmon fishing provided the best vacation and experience of my life, respectively. I am so thankful that I kept my promise.

My Alaskan experience taught me a very valuable lesson; I never promise anything unless I am sure I can follow through. My word is golden. I cannot say that this has always been true for me; but this valuable lesson will remain part of who I am for the rest of my life. If you want to be respected, it is important to keep and honor your commitments.

When people depend on you, honor your commitments, and do what you are supposed to do. Make sure you follow through, whether you are dealing with your family, friends, job, paying your debts, returning borrowed items, or any other facet of your life. My mom always used to say, "Don't borrow unless it is absolutely necessary, but if you must, make sure you return the item clean and in a better condition than when you borrowed it." It's like paying a little interest.

You keep a promise when repaying a promissory note, you pay the amount borrowed but you also pay the added interest. I'm shocked when I hear individuals talk about abusing rental cars and/or rental equipment. I wonder how they would like it if they owned the rental company. Guess what? The cost is passed on to the consumer. Now it doesn't take a rocket scientist to figure that one out, but I hear this kind of talk all the time.

People who keep their promises are dependable, punctual, and they are prepared. My rule is that if you are on time, you are fifteen minutes early. Being prepared, whether it is homework, a presentation, or just showing up for work appropriately dressed and ready to put in an honest day's work, is the fulfillment of the promise we make for the reward we receive, whether it is a grade, a paycheck, or a promotion. Individuals who keep their promises do not make excuses. Remember, most excuses are lies!

Finally, keeping promises to your family and loved ones is vital for nurturing strong flourishing relationships. It is our moral duty to be a person of character, one our family, friends, and those in authority can depend on to fulfill our commitments. If you want to have great relationships, your character will make or break you. "Be true in all words and actions."[12]

Practice your self-talk, create your mental imagery, and monitor your actions.

Every Day Say:

- I always keep my promises.
- I never promise anything that I cannot fulfill.
- I stop and think before I make promises.
- My word is golden.
- People can depend on me.
- I always do what I say I will do.

Hopefully, you are now in the habit of stressing each important word in the saying. Again, keep in mind The Rule of Thirty Days says if you miss a day you have to start over again.

The reason I say this is because I know it works! After watching my son, Tom, try over and over to quit smoking, his thirty day positive affirmations did the trick after thirty-five years of smoking. Tom had tried several times to quit smoking, but in each case he was unsuccessful. Ironically, he wasn't sure the thirty days would work so he bought nicotine patches. After two days he said, "I don't know why I spent money on these patches because *I don't smoke.*" He used the patches for the first two days and never used them again. It has been months since he quit smoking and he still refuses to say, "I quit smoking." Instead, he still says his positive affirmation, "I don't smoke."

Create a mental image of you making a promise to a friend, just as I did when I promised Marilyn I would visit her in Alaska. Now, picture yourself as a mouse in the corner watching your friend's reaction and expression as she discovers, you have broken the promise. Repeat this scenario, but this time you have kept the promise. Next, put yourself in your friend's shoes, and really feel her emotion. Come up with some other mental pictures that fit other statements of your self-talk. Envision yourself as the person you want to become.

Watch what you promise, and commit to each day, and monitor your actions carefully. In the evening evaluate yourself. Always, make sure to give yourself praise for a job well done. Even if you slip up to a degree, ask yourself if you are a better person today than you were in the past. If you can say, "Yes," you are deserving of praise. In life, growth in personal development is essential if you want to be successful; you must keep pushing yourself forward by asking yourself tough questions. That is why you ask yourself questions like, "What can I do to improve?" "What could I have done differently that would have been more constructive or provided a better outcome?" "What can I do tomorrow?"

RELIABILITY

"I will keep my word...and upon all occasions shall speak the truth, though I sometimes tell it at my own expense."[13]

Have you ever had someone say they would pick you up at a certain time to attend an event or to take you to work? How did you feel about that person when they were late or didn't show up at all? What did you think of their excuses? I'm sure you thought that so and so is the most unreliable...(You fill in the blank)

                                    MARJORIE BARCOMB

Reliable people are consistent in their behaviors. You know where they are coming from. They are not wishy-washy nor a flip flopper. Reliable people stand up for the right thing all the time. When you are reliable, you do what you say you are going to do whether it is working on or attending an event, doing your homework, or household chores, etc. Are you always on time? Do you do good job? Don't make people worry; make your words and actions consistent and true. Are you always a reliable person? If the answer is, "Yes," excellent! If you said, "Sometimes," the practice below will help you to change your answer to, "Yes!"

Practice your self-talk, practice your mental imagery, and monitor your actions.

Every Day Say:

- I always say what I mean and I mean what I say.
- I am always on time.
- I am consistent in my behaviors.
- I don't make people worry.

Stress each important word and keep in mind 'The Rule of Thirty Days!'

Picture yourself being the first person entering the room for an important meeting; you have all your important papers with you, and you are ready for the meeting. How does it feel to be the first person in the room? What do you think your boss will think of you? Think of some other scenarios that fit what you do in your daily regimen. Conjure up the emotion of feeling so worthwhile being on time—all the time. People can depend on you!

Check your actions each day and evaluate yourself on your reliability. Continue doing this until you see the behavior you would expect from a highly successful person. Remember, Rome wasn't built in a day. Your progress is to be praised even if it is in small increments!

TRUSTWORTHINESS

> "Trust each other again and again. When the trust level gets high enough, people transcend apparent limits, discovering new and awesome abilities for which they were previously unaware."[14]

People who are not trustworthy are hypocrites. They cannot be counted on in any setting. People who can be trusted stand up for what they believe in no matter how much it may hurt or what the consequences of their actions yield. They ascribe to the standards that we have already covered. We all like to be trusted. We like to work with people who are trustworthy; we want trustworthy people as our friends, neighbors, and associates. Most of all we want our family members to be trustworthy. That is the only way we can help each other to the fullest extent. It is our moral duty to be trustworthy. "The man of integrity walks securely, but he who takes crooked paths will be found out."[15]

Practice your self-talk, create your mental images, and monitor your actions.

Every Day Say:

- I can always be trusted.
- I like to work with trustworthy people.
- I want only trustworthy people as my friends.

- It is my moral duty to be trustworthy.

Practice your mental imagery. Picture yourself surrounded by friends who are all extremely trustworthy. You may have to make up new friends for this scene. You don't have to worry about any false statements, or any other integrity flaws. You don't have to pick and choose your words for fear they will be misinterpreted or become part of someone's gossip session. How does it feel?

Watch your actions to make sure that everything you do would be characteristic of a trustworthy person. Evaluate yourself each evening. What does your assessment tell you? Don't forget to praise yourself for even the smallest improvement and never give up!

FORGIVENESS AND RECONCILIATION SET YOU FREE

"Teach me to feel another's woe, to hide the fault I see; that mercy I to others show, that mercy show to me."[1]

Have you ever wondered why some people seem to be angry all the time, whereas others never seem to get angry no matter what the circumstances are? The difference is that some have learned how to control their anger and/or have learned to analyze the source of their displeasure. Generally, people who make you angry have their own set of problems, and some cope by lashing out at others. Shouldn't they be pitied rather than being the target of your revenge? Sometimes we have a real right to be angry when we have been wronged unfairly, but we must consider how the consequences of our anger affect us. Conflict is inevitable, but your response is your choice.

Other times there is only a perceived wrong, and the anger has no basis in fact. Frequently anger is a learned behavior, a behavior that has been modeled over and over by care givers and others as well as behaviors that have gone unchecked in the individual. Just as anger is learned, controlling anger can be learned. You cannot be angry and in conflict and be happy and peaceful at the same time.

Why would you be willing to suffer the consequences of anger when distress, hostility, enslavement, illness, and bitterness are the destructive by-products? Are you willing to pay such a price? Of course not! So what's the answer?

The only answer that frees us from the bondage of anger is forgiveness and reconciliation. You may say, "Well I can forgive, but I can't reconcile." Let's start with forgiveness. True forgiveness means that you are willing to give up wanting revenge or that "So and so needs to pay." It isn't always easy to forgive, but it is in forgiving that we are set free. It's the only answer. As long as you harbor bitterness, hurt, or pain from someone's wrongdoing, it is you that suffers, not the perpetrator. Are you going to let them continue to torture you? It doesn't make sense!

Some people are angry and know why, whereas others are angry and don't even know why. Anger is described as a strong feeling of intense displeasure or uneasiness which causes immense chemical changes in the body and nervous system. This abnormal body chemistry causes stress, depression, emotional distress, as well as mental and physical illness. Who would want to torture themselves in this way?

Some people have borne burdens from pain inflicted by others that seem almost impossible to bear, much less to forgive; therefore, there are many obstacles standing in the way of their freedom. It is hard for me to conceive forgiveness by someone who has lost a child to a sexual-predator, but some people have worked through heartbreaks like this and have found freedom from the bondage of hate and bitterness. They have learned that the lack of forgiveness hurts them, not the criminal. Maybe the perpetrator should not be forgiven; but is the result worth it?

There are many obstacles to forgiving—pride, fear, partial forgiveness, listening to others, re-living the incident over and over again and therefore, not willing to let go, or being just plain obstinate and unwilling to forgive. There are people who prefer to wallow in their pain than to forgive. This is a sad testimony about humanity.

Pride is the greatest of all sins; therefore, some people are just too proud to forgive. That is not pride; that is a self-destructive behavior. Asking for forgiveness is a sign of strength. It shows that you are willing to go the extra mile to live a life free from stress and bondage.

Fear of what the other person involved might say or think will stop many from granting or asking for forgiveness. They fear that the other person will think they are weak. They fear that the other person will reject their granting of forgiveness or plea for forgiveness. If the other person does any of these things, shame on them, not on you!

Nothing short of full and total forgiveness, without conditions, limitations, or demands, works. A little bit of forgiveness is like a little bit dead. It's all or nothing. You are either dead or you are not; you either forgive or you do not. You can't just hold on to some anger and let some go. If you try that, you are still in bondage. But what if you just don't know where to get started, the hurt is so deep. Your magnificent brain will help you with this one. "True forgiveness includes total acceptance. And out of acceptance, wounds are healed and happiness is possible again."[2]

Listening to others wanting you to hang on to your onus is destructive. It is not they who suffer the stress and damage caused by bitterness and lack of forgiveness. Listen to your own conscience. It is you who has to live with your conscience, your health issues, and your life.

Some people like to dwell on the wrongdoing, and repeat it over and over in their mind every day. They seem to love their misery or just can't seem to get past the incident. Rehearsing the incident over and over makes it more and more difficult to let go and let healing begin. When destructive thoughts come to mind, you should sit down and start writing all the things you should be thankful for. A thankfulness journal has helped many people to get past many of life's dilemmas. Finally, there those who just plain do not want to forgive, no matter what the benefits of forgiveness are. If you try to convince them that forgiveness is the best medicine, it seems as though you are talking to a post. What is important here is that you have planted a seed. It may sprout later on when the soil is more fertile. The richness of the human brain is beyond description and your seed may change a life.

Well, where do you start on your road to forgiveness? Practice. Practice. Practice. Do a little role playing. Grant forgiveness or ask for forgiveness silently at first, then practice saying it out loud–over and over (thirty consecutive days). Looking in a mirror as you practice really helps. It gets easier as time goes on. We must confess our anger, hostility, bitterness, resentment, and rage–even if it is just to the mirror. Eventually, you will start to let go of the hurt, the bitter feelings and the resentment of having been wronged. Hopefully, the time will come when you are at a point of just more than saying it—you actually have moved

                                    MARJORIE BARCOMB

it from your lips to your heart, and can now tell the other person that you forgive them for what they have done and maybe even ask for their forgiveness for harboring such bitterness and resentment towards them. Freedom!

Forgiveness is not easy, but it is one of the most unselfish acts you can perform. It's good to remember that we have all done things for which we need forgiveness, and really appreciate it when someone forgives us. It is our responsibility to initiate forgiveness.

When we forgive, harsh feelings are replaced by compassion. In our reconciliation, we learn to accept others the way they are, or in some cases we must separate ourselves from them. In either case the forgiveness is essential, and the freedom from bondage and resentment caused by anger is worth the effort. When looking at the greatest trials and heartaches of your life, love and forgiveness are the healing forces that get you through and reinstate the joy in your heart that should be rightfully yours.

An amazing example of the healing power that true forgiveness provides is found in the story of Jennifer Thompson-Cannino and Ronald Cotton.[3] The book they co-authored, *Picking Cotton: Our Memoir of Injustice and Redemption,* details their account. Jennifer, a rape victim, picked Ronald Cotton out of a physical line-up and also from a photograph as the rapist. Unfortunately, the real perpetrator had an amazing resemblance to the innocent Cotton. Cotton spent eleven years in prison for a crime he did not commit. Every day he was in prison, Jennifer prayed that he'd be raped and killed in prison. Finally, with the advent of DNA testing, Cotton asked his attorney if any of the crime scene evidence was still available for DNA testing. By the grace of God, a small amount of semen was available, and the DNA showed that the true rapist, who was already serving time for another rape, was Bobby Poole.

Jennifer's guilt brought her to ask for a meeting with Ronald Cotton where she said that even if she said she was sorry every minute, every hour, every day of the rest of her life, it couldn't compare with what she felt in her heart. Ronald forgave her immediately. Their families have become close friends; they have co-authored a book and travel the country giving presentations about their history. Many blessings have been bestowed on both families and those they touch through their words because of true forgiveness. They looked beyond the conflict to the opportunity to fulfill their life's purpose. Even though they faced the greatest trials and heartaches in their lives, love and forgiveness were the healing forces that got them through and reinstated joy in their hearts.

"A person should not be ashamed to own he has been in the wrong, which is like saying, in other words, that he is wiser today than he was yesterday."[4] Besides that, forgiveness is our responsibility.

Practice your self-talk, practice your mental imagery, and monitor your actions.

Every Day Say:

- I have a forgiving nature.
- I work on forgiveness every day.
- I am not afraid to ask for forgiveness.
- I am not too proud to ask for forgiveness.

- I am strong; therefore, I forgive.
- I want to forgive.
- Forgiveness sets me free.
- True forgiveness eliminates stress.
- True forgiveness eliminates physical ailments.
- True forgiveness eliminates emotional turmoil.

Remember the Rule of Thirty Days says that if you miss a day you have to start over again.

Think of someone who has wronged you in some way. Get a clear picture of him or her in your mind. Do you feel grief and turmoil? Try to understand that the person you are thinking about may be carrying around very destructive messages in his or her subconscious, and if so, may not have a lot of control over their actions. Don't suffer another second because of the destructive behavior exhibited by others. Find a nice quiet place and start working on your forgiveness. Picture the turmoil that must be going on in the other person. Feel his or her anguish. Now, picture yourself forgiving him/her. First, picture yourself thinking that you must forgive to stop your own hurt. Then picture yourself thinking, "I forgive so and so. Next picture yourself saying out loud, "I forgive you." Finally, picture yourself talking to so and so saying, "I forgive you for what you did or said to me." You do this not because he or she is a gentleman or a lady but because you are. Please understand that this process may take days, weeks, and even months. Don't give up; the outcome is worth it. The significant spin off is your freedom from the bondage of the torment that you have allowed.

Spend the next few days following up by watching

your actions with respect to those who have wronged you. For example, let's assume that someone at your workplace has hurt you, and you haven't forgiven him or her. A simple "good morning" to someone whom you haven't spoken to because of the lack of forgiveness on your part is a good start. They may desperately want your forgiveness. Remember you must forgive if you expect to be forgiven. Each evening ponder your progress. Give yourself a really big pat on the back if you have started on your forgiveness.

RESPECT FOR SELF, OTHERS AND THE ENVIRONMENT PROVIDES FOR TEAMWORK AND BUILDS STRONG PERSONAL RELATIONSHIPS

*"Without feelings of respect,
what is there to distinguish
people from beasts?"*[1]

RESPECT FOR SELF

"A person that has self-respect is safe from others. That person wears a coat of armor that none can pierce."[2]

You cannot have the respect of others unless you respect yourself. Self-respect is a necessary ingredient in your arsenal of personal virtues that will take you over the mountains and through the valleys of your life. Your self-respect is a cornerstone in the foundation of your life. If your self-respect is in the tank, no matter how hard you work at accomplishing anything in life, you quite possibly will fail. In the chapters that follow, you will learn how to pull yourself up out of the tank; it is so easy, I wish I had learned how to do so years ago.

Many personal attributes fall under self-respect such as self-discipline and physical, mental, emotional, and spiritual health habits. All lead to the development of strong ethical relationships that enhance your life.

Individuals who lack self-respect are easily led, and in looking to others for guidance, frequently fall into a trap of learned helplessness or hopelessness or worse yet, a life of crime. They frequently become mired in a self-pitying mode. They often lash out at others whom they think are successful, and they seem to enjoy making others as miserable as they are. It's a long hard climb from this type of abyss, but with dedication and practice it can be done. And the most hopeless of us can dig our way out and become self-respecting, happy, productive individuals, and may even become leaders in our society. The key here is the willingness to make changes, no matter how difficult the climb may seem.

If you respect yourself, you care about yourself. You are your own best friend. You want to feel good about who you are, how you present yourself, and how you appear to others. You want people to see you as a person of value or worth. You want to be an ethical person with a good reputation. Your self-respect is frequently exhibited in your caring about others, especially those close to you.

I find it mind-boggling how some individuals have a totally different personality when it comes to their immediate family as compared to others. I've seen people treat their spouses with disdain while treating their co-workers with great respect. A person who does this is only interested in their reputation and not in their character. Remember your reputation is what people think you are, and your character is what you really are. Do you want to merely be a person with a good reputation, or do you want to be a person of good character? If you have good character, your good reputation is sure to follow since one of the major spin offs of good character is a good reputation.

To be sought by others and to feel good about your worth, there are things you must do. You must be in control of many aspects of your life. You must also strive for and nurture life-long learning in the area of personal development. You must seek, cherish, and nurture strong ethical personal relationships; enjoy your leisure time; monitor your behavior; and seek improvement.

SELF-DISCIPLINE/SELF-CONTROL

> "Self-respect is the fruit of discipline; the sense of
> dignity grows with the ability to say no to oneself."[3]

Controlling many facets of your life or self-discipline doesn't come easily, but as in any business, management is of utmost importance. Managing and controlling your actions maximizes your self-worth. Controlling anger, controlling your temper, and controlling your words require a lot of self-discipline. The role models that you had as you were growing up play a significant part in how much control you may seem to have over your life now. The key is to control yourself and not to control others. Don't be a control freak!

Controlling anger allows you to take charge of your life and your environment. We all know how uncomfortable and distressing it is to be in the vicinity of an angry or frustrated person. Some of you may have endured years of disrespect and lived at the mercy of a caregiver or a spouse who constantly attacked you verbally over instances that a normal person would overlook or even laugh at. We have all come from diverse backgrounds; therefore, it is important that in respecting yourself, you understand that not everyone has had the same life experiences you have had. The consequence is that it is okay for people to have different likes and dislikes. You do not need to seek to control anyone else into liking or believing as you do by screaming, threatening, or intimidating. Respect yourself and others enough to make sure this doesn't happen due to your own insecurity or just plain being out of control. When it comes to family disagreements, control your anger, especially in front of others. Bite your tongue so to speak. Save family issues for private family discussions; otherwise, you put others in a very awkward position. It is a great feeling when you know you could have blown up or gotten angry but you were able to control the situation as a result of behaving as a self-controlled mature adult. Often the perceived offense doesn't seem quite as bad when you give yourself a little time to cool off, and then you can discuss the incident or situation rationally. Most people are not very rational when they are angry.

Personally, when I'm confronted with a stressful situation, I ask myself, "Can I live with this for an hour? … a day? … a week? … a month?" Then depending on the answer, I wait. Guess what? Ninety-nine percent of the time the issue has been resolved before I have to address it. If the issue needs to be addressed after the appropriate wait time, I can do it with a cool head and do it rationally. Using this model prevents expending a lot of unnecessary energy, but more importantly it prevents stress. Any self-respecting person would not want to waste their energy on stressful situations that could be solved independent of their input or, better yet, totally avoided.

An example of how this process works occurred when I received a nasty voice message on my cell phone from a committee member. Even though the comments weren't directed at me, I was shocked. I was so taken aback that I hurriedly punched in seven to delete the message. After a second or two had passed, I asked myself, "Can I live without responding to this today?" "Can I live with it for a week?" My answer was, "Yes!" After two weeks had passed, the committee had to meet again. I was able to conduct the meeting with a confident air and a positive demeanor and to treat the other committee member as a gentleman—not because he was a gentleman, but because I was a lady.

Controlling your words is another area of concern when it comes to self-respect and/or self-worth. I hear individuals cutting others to shreds with their tongue as if with a freshly sharpened sword. I hear spouses screaming, calling each other very nasty names, and using profane language. I hear belittling in the workplace. I hear some parents using nothing but negative language when talking to their children. I hear tons of gossip. All of these are very hurtful and destructive behaviors, and anyone who ascribes even a little bit to any of these out of control aspects of civility, not only injures others but they injure themselves as well. Their self-respect suffers dramatically. Spread sunshine, not darkness, and your self-worth will grow in leaps and bounds. Do this daily!

The mouth seems to be the center of many problems. Remember we were born with two ears and one mouth. That's for a reason!! We should listen twice as much as we talk. We should be slow to speak, and when we do, we should choose our words thoughtfully and carefully to insure they do not injure anyone. "Fill people's lives with sweetness. Speak approving, cheering words while their ears can hear them, and while their hearts can be thrilled and made happier by them."[4] Giving praise is like giving a bouquet of flowers, it fills the air with a sweet aroma. "I praise loudly. I blame softly."[5]

Another area of self-control deals with our ego. I'm sure you've met people with a super-sized ego. Don't they make you want to run? Through the years, I have come to understand that most people who appear to have a big ego or those who need their ego stroked all the time suffer from low self-esteem and from a need to feel accepted and/or cherished. That is very unfortunate, but we must all rise above our faults and circumstances. That is the precise reason that I am writing this book–to help people rise above their past. You will learn how to make these changes in subsequent chapters. After reading this book, you may feel that you are doing just fine; some of you may get some pointers on how to improve upon certain facets of your life; and for others this book may spawn a life-changing experience. That is my hope for you! As a bonus, it may help you to understand the actions of others.

My advice is to guard your reputation and your character by guarding your words. Everyone is worthwhile, and those who mean something to you already know that you are. You do not have to brag or stretch the truth to be noticed or accepted by those who don't care. They won't care anyway, so don't give them fodder to gossip about you. By making your personal development a life-long learning objective, you won't have to worry about accolades because your heart will be filled with joy just being who you are and who you are becoming.

Self-respect also includes controlling your finances. Many changes have occurred in this country over time. The advent of easy borrowing via credit cards has ruined many people and many families. The credit card companies really don't care how many sleepless nights you spend because you have over-extended yourself financially. Take a look at your credit card bill, and if you don't have one, ask someone else if you can look at one of their old credit card bills. Look at the amount of interest owed for the month and the amount of the minimum payment. You may find that the interest is more than half of the minimum payment which means that you are paying more in interest than you are paying on the principal. Imagine that! If you continue using the credit card and paying the minimum payment, you are paying more than twice the price of every product or service that you are receiving. Wouldn't you be kinder to yourself if you just paid the price for a product one time? I know, I know, there are a lot of excuses as to why, "I had to!"

There were many benefits to *not* having credit cards when I was a child. People just waited until they had enough money to buy products, and they just paid for them once. Now, people who are addicted to credit cards and pay the minimum payment could have much more buying power if they just waited until they could pay cash. The other great benefit of controlling your finances is getting a good night's sleep. You, too, can become fiscally responsible.

Let me give you another example that just blows me out of the water. It is the out of control spending on the part of almost every homeowner with the burden of a thirty year mortgage. Even though your mortgage bill shows what you are paying in interest and what is being paid on the principal, the actual dollar amount you pay in the first twenty-one years is equal to your interest. In the last nine years what you pay is equal to your principal. Everyone is brainwashed into the deception that they have to have everything right now! They need their dream home right now! Several years ago, I recall listening to Larry Burkett in a radio program called, Money Matters, and I was amazed at his suggestion about home mortgages. He suggested that you buy a home that you can pay off in seven years (you'd probably have to finance it for ten and calculate what it would take to pay it off in seven). Yes, I know, this is not your dream home, but at the end of seven years the home and its equity is completely yours. Now you can sell that home and use your sale price as a down payment on an upgraded home that you again pay off in seven years. At the end of that seven years, now a total of fourteen years, you have paid off two homes, and now after selling this home, you have the money for a big down payment to buy much more than your original dream home, and you will pay it off in another seven years. So at the end of twenty-one years you have paid off a home that is nicer than your original dream home that you wanted to finance for thirty years. Remember that with the

                    MARJORIE BARCOMB

thirty year mortgage you would have spent enough money in the first twenty-one years to just pay off the interest. You would still owe an amount equal to the entire original principal of your dream home. Why is a little sacrifice up front so unimaginable? It is important to always think for yourself on every issue.

Self-respect doesn't mean you have to own a hot car; it means you own a car you can afford. I was looking at a car contract recently on a $34,000 vehicle and it ended up costing the purchaser $58,000. This included the taxes, a low interest rate and, of course, it included all the extra warranties the car salesman talked the individual into buying. Think through your purchases and don't buy on impulse. If you should happen to buy a big ticket item on impulse, you generally have a seventy-two hour buyer's remorse window to renege. Don't be too proud to take back a big ticket item. Your self-esteem will suffer for just a few days, but with a six or seven year car contract that you can barely afford, your self-esteem will endure the sting for the duration of the contract. Indebtedness erodes your self-respect and robs your joy.

For many individuals, financial problems stem from a lack of control with respect to their worldly desires. Controlling human desires and appetites is of paramount significance when it comes to self-discipline, self control, or self-respect because the consequences can have an overpowering effect on your self-worth and your general health. The following merit your scrutiny: control the consumption of alcohol, control the use of tobacco and drugs both legal and illegal, control gambling and other gaming addictions, control the amount of food and the kinds of food you eat, and control your sexual appetite. Misuse or overuse of any of these desires can cause irreversible damage to your self-worth and your health. All can lead to illness, crime, and/or even death. I think we all have succumbed and let our desires take over at one time or another in our lives, but that doesn't mean that we have to continue down that path of destruction. Let's take a closer look.

Alcohol has caused deaths and injuries due to car accidents, crime due to personality changes, and diseases such as cirrhosis of the liver. Everyone wants you to have a good time, but in the process, be sure that you plan ahead. If you intend to consume any alcohol whatsoever, have a designated driver. Many people exhibit personality changes when they consume alcohol. Some get funny, some get quiet, some get giggly, some get sleepy, and some get mean. Fighting, arguing, and domestic violence are highly correlated with the degree of alcohol consumption. Over-all, if you plan to consume alcohol, it is best to use it sparingly.

Smoking increases the probability of cancer and heart disease. Although it is legal, nicotine is an exceedingly addictive drug, and as a consequence, many smokers wish they had never started. Smoking constricts small blood vessels; that's why you see premature wrinkling in smokers. Smokers miss more work, and have more medical claims than individuals who do not smoke. Besides, smokers don't smell very good. They don't know it, but the rest of us do. If you don't smoke, don't start. If you do smoke, quit! Get the glow back in your skin, smell clean, and get healthier. Wow, that's a no brainer!

Many people die each year from drug overdoses, both prescribed and illegal. If at all possible stay away from prescription drugs except in cases of absolute necessity. It is much better to concentrate on health and wellness to circumvent illness. The great thing about having health and wellness as a major focus in your life is, that it lets you enjoy your life. No one wants pain and suffering!

Illegal drugs are closely tied with drug trafficking and violence. Border Patrol Agents, policeman and other drug enforcement agents have succumbed at the hands of drug traffickers, drug lords, and drug cartel members. Many unenlightened individuals all the way from a novice who has tried a drug just once to seriously addicted drug users find themselves ill, hospitalized, or in their grave. If you find yourself in any of these categories, get help immediately!

Overeating and improper nutrition have contributed to the increase in obesity in America which in turn has caused a dramatic increase in diabetes, premature deaths, and other related illnesses. Insurance claims for obese individuals have sky-rocketed as a result. Obese individuals desperately need proper nutrition and exercise. Again, if you suffer from obesity, get the help you need. Hopefully, as you continue reading this book you will find many ideas that can help you on your journey to successful weight loss and ultimately, weight maintenance.

Sexual crimes against children and sexual deviancy are at an all time high. Loose sexual mores have contributed to an exponential increase in the number and occurrence of sexually transmitted diseases. It seems that people have been brain-washed into believing that instant gratification is better than delayed gratification enjoyed as a result of a respectful, nurturing, and loving relationship. What is your body worth? I'd say, a lot, enough to make sure you are not being exploited by anyone.

Your body is the structure you live in while you are on earth, and you should take care of it. Control your appearance by dressing appropriately for the occasion. If you want people to respect you, dress accordingly. It's no wonder that some people complain about the way they are treated when they dress like an exhibitionist or like someone who doesn't care what they look like. You don't have to be rich to have decent clean clothing.

Another element of your appearance is your personal hygiene and grooming habits. Take a hard look at your overall appearance and rate yourself on your hair, nails, skin, etc. I think we could all find some area in which improvement could be advantageous. I'm not saying that we need to be high maintenance–I'm saying that most of us can do a lot to improve our appearance without spending a lot of money. Just a little attention to detail works! Aren't you worth it?

Finally, control your time. Many things are wasted in America, but the most costly waste is the waste of time. People who seem to accomplish ten times more than anyone else use their calendars and schedule their activities. They write down their goals and objectives. They make lists and prioritize what needs to be done. Then they get to work. They don't spend hours each day on the couch watching television or sitting in front of their computers playing solitaire. Subsequent chapters will show you how

                                    MARJORIE BARCOMB

to get organized which will ultimately assist you in controlling your time.

Your self-discipline as measured by controlling yourself in many facets of your life can make your life much more pleasant and build your confidence; both will lead to long term success and happiness. If you want your self-respect to increase dramatically, look at the areas that drag you down; then proactively start your positive self-talk regimen to build new neural pathways for improving your life in these areas.

HEALTH AND WELLNESS

"He who has health has hope; and he who has hope has everything."[6]

When a person respects themselves, they take good care of their body, mind, and spirit. It is in being healthy physically, mentally, emotionally, and spiritually, that we can accomplish great feats, fulfill our dreams, and live happy, fruitful lives. Feeling great, accomplishing much, and loving our life is a great recipe for increased self-worth. Let's take a look at each of these concepts.

What does it take to strive for good physical health? My many years of experience on this planet lead me to the conclusion that after the need for shelter, we need water, proper nutrition, exercise and sleep. Each of these is immensely central when it comes to a healthy lifestyle.

The combination of our hereditary factors and lifestyle contribute collectively to produce cofactors that work together to cause our illnesses and diseases. There is no single cause of any health problem. Causative cofactors work together synergistically like pieces of a complex puzzle to promote a chain of events ending with health problems manifested as symptoms, disease, or illness. Modern medicine, in a simplistic way, blames too many problems on our genetics, bacteria, and/or viruses. We are complex human beings; therefore, our health issues are complex. We are all different and the same set of cofactors can be manifested as different conditions in different individuals. Conversely, different people can be diagnosed with the same illness with an entirely different set of cofactors causing that same illness. Every person is different! Every individual lives a different life! Give two people lemons. One makes a sour face and the other smiles and makes lemonade.

Our genetics represent our predisposition to develop a health problem or disease. Our lifestyle is the prime determinant as to whether or not we are going to experience an illness or disease. All diseases or illnesses are multidimensional and are not caused by single factor! Anything that disturbs the balance inside our body, our mind, and our spirit from being in harmony with our environment will lead to health issues and promote illness.

This is a wake-up call for all of us to do our best to eliminate stress, think positive thoughts, eat nutritional foods, detoxify our bodies, have consistent sleep for eight to nine hours each night, and exercise several times each week. Forgive and laugh a lot!

Many of the foods that are available today are not exactly stellar when it comes to proper nutrition. (But a little chocolate is allowed!) It's unfortunate in a time of such great affluence in this country that many are undernourished. Our farmland has been depleted of many essential nutrients; therefore, our crops yield fruit and vegetables with inadequate nutritional content. Many fast foods contain an abundance of trans-fats and sodium. If you look around, you can see that most of us do not need more fat and salt. I feel that many people are overweight because they are starving for some deficiency in their diet. When we have a deficiency, we eat more because it comes across as hunger. Whether we are overweight, underweight, or at an acceptable weight, most of us need to supplement our diet with nutritional-supplements that contain essential vitamins and minerals to enhance our health.

Another dietary problem is that of eating too many refined, preserved, and processed foods. The ingestion of too many preservatives and the lack of fiber are just two factors that result in many intestinal problems and diseases. We should get totally away from processed foods; the preservatives scare me. These two factors contribute to the wiping out of the good flora in the intestine that aids in digestion and elimination. Enteric coated pro-biotics (beneficial bacteria) seem to help many people to repopulate the good bacteria in their intestinal tracts. We should cook and eat the way our great-grandmother cooked and ate.

Autopsies have shown that many people die with ten to forty pounds of plaque stuck like spackle or paste inside their intestines. This is toxic! Between eating problem foods and inhaling pesticides, etc. in the air we breathe, we are indeed toxic. Our entire bodies need to be detoxified. How do we do this? Many people have been successful using herbal detox tea, herbal colon-cleanse, and other natural seven-day detox regimens.

Dehydration is another cause of health issues. To make sure that you are drinking enough water, take your body weight and divide that number by two. For example, if you weigh 150 pounds, 150/2=75. That means that you should drink seventy-five ounces of water each day. That does not mean seventy-five ounces of soda pop or coffee. It means seventy-five ounces of water. And while we are on the subject, regular sodas contain several tablespoons of sugar, and diet sodas contain artificial sweeteners that even the ants won't eat. Dr. D'Adamo, author of, *Eat Right 4 Your Type*, states that these artificial sweeteners actually slow your metabolism.[7] They are metabolic inhibitors. Not a good trade-off! Besides, aren't we smarter than ants? Drink water—get healthy. If you are an adult and you wait until you are thirsty to drink, you are already dehydrated.

Your mental and emotional health is synergistically tied to your physical health. We spoke before of cofactors determining your state of health and well-being. Your physical health, therefore, is a major player in the degree of emotional and mental health you enjoy. Your emotional health can be promoted in many ways and being physically healthy is a critical component.

Good physical health coming from proper nutrition, exercise, and adequate sleep may be the best medicine for good emotional and mental health unless someone has a serious mental or emotional disorder. Much new research in the area of brain chemistry and disorders is now available. Consequently, there is a lot more help for people who

                    MARJORIE BARCOMB

have these serious conditions than there has been in the past.

Emotional downs are tough and sometimes people need counseling. Counseling is not a quick fix! It takes time for emotional healing in many cases. There is professional help out there, and when individuals are in very tough emotional distress, they should seek help.

In situations where you may be a bit down because things just don't seem to be going your way, setting goals, reading inspirational stories, finding a role model or mentor, and meditation may be the answer.

Surround yourself with positive people, and separate yourself from negative people. Negative people are an anchor that drags you down. When the negative people are in your own family, you need to tell them that you are not interested in their negativity and do not appreciate their dumping on you. Then walk away! When you associate with positive people, you become enlightened and your self-concept improves. Get around the right people. Get around positive, successful people. Associate with men and women who are going somewhere with their lives. And get away from negative, critical, complaining people. They drag you down, tire you out, distract, and discourage you, and lead you inevitably to underachievement and failure.

Remember, "You cannot fly with the eagles if you continue to scratch with the turkeys."[8]

Positive people are not always available when we are down. That is why I suggest that everyone have a thankfulness journal in which to write all the things you are thankful for each day. It's remarkable how writing in such a journal can change how you feel in just a few days! Even though you definitely will encounter difficult situations, overall, we live in the greatest nation on earth and have unprecedented freedom. No one in any other country enjoys our degree of freedom. Now that's something to be thankful for.

Some people cannot ignore their spiritual health whether they have been raised by parents or care-givers with a religious background or not. It is important to know where to turn when these individuals need help. I suggest going to your clergy or someone you can trust who you believe to be a spiritual person to give you a sense of direction—a first step. Then I suggest that you read, study, and make up your own mind as to what you believe. As a Christian, I feel that it is my duty to tell you to read and study about this matter. We don't want you drinking the cool-aid. If you don't understand that expression, look up Jim Jones and the Jonestown Massacre.

Your physical health, emotional and mental health, and your spiritual health are all of great significance in cultivating and maintaining your self-respect and self-worth. Guard your health in all that you do. Have fun, but don't take any unnecessary chances that could hurt you in any way. You have to finish reading the book!

Practice your self-talk, practice your mental imagery, and monitor your actions.

Life is all about choices. Look at the list below, and find where you would like to make changes in your life. Feel free to add or amend any that apply to you. Conversely, feel free to delete those that do not apply to you. I cannot stress strongly enough the significance of your doing this for the thirty consecutive days.

Every Day Say:

- I am not easily led.
- I can think for myself.
- I am willing to make changes.
- I care about myself.
- I am a valuable person.
- I enjoy being an ethical person.
- I value my good reputation.
- I am a person of good character.
- I control my anger.
- I control my temper.
- I choose my words thoughtfully.
- I listen intently.
- I listen twice as much as I talk.
- I give praise to someone every day.
- I do not brag about my accomplishments.
- I do not stretch the truth.
- I do not gossip.
- I praise loudly.
- I do not belittle anyone.
- I spread sunshine.
- I smile a lot.
- People like me.
- I am a good person.
- I am worthwhile.
- I pay my bills on time.
- I don't buy anything I can't afford.

- I don't buy on impulse.
- I don't use credit cards.
- I wait until I can pay cash.
- I control my consumption of alcohol.
- I do not drink alcohol.
- I do not drink more than one drink per day.
- I do not smoke.
- I do not do any illegal drugs.
- I only take prescription drugs when it is absolutely necessary.
- I do not gamble.
- I do not over-eat.
- I do not eat junk foods or foods with preservatives.
- I eat a balanced diet.
- I supplement my diet with vitamins and minerals.
- I exercise 4 times per week.
- I do not participate in illicit sexual activity.
- I dress appropriately for the occasion.
- I do not dress like a bum.
- I do not dress like an exhibitionist.
- I control my time.
- I do not waste time.
- I plan ahead.
- I use my calendar.
- I am organized.
- I am confident.
- I go out of my way to eliminate stress.
- I think positive thoughts.
- I detoxify my body.
- I forgive.

- I smile and laugh a lot.
- I sleep at least eight hours each night.
- I drink the required number of ounces of water each day.
- I am thankful every day.
- I write in my thankfulness journal each day.
- I set goals.
- I read inspirational stories.
- I go to church every…
- I read the Bible every…
- I nurture my spiritual health by…

I know that I have been talking about the Rule of Thirty Days, but it doesn't hurt to review and repeat these self-talk statements, coupled with those you come up with, throughout your future.

Again, there are so many possibilities when it comes to mental imaging about your self-respect; volumes could be written. In the area of health and wellness for example, picture yourself drinking the appropriate amount of water each day. You could see yourself getting up at six o'clock a.m., drinking water, eight o'clock a.m., drinking water and so on throughout the day on the even hour. If you needed eighty ounces of water, or eight ten ounce glasses of water each day, by drinking ten ounces of water on the even hour, you could start at six o'clock a.m. and end at eight o'clock p.m. Picture yourself doing this, and you will find your brain helping you—you will somehow find yourself looking at the clock on the even hour or very close to it.

Whatever you have decided to do today, dealing with your self-respect, monitor your actions. If you decided to use the drinking water example of mental imagery, you are ready for action. Make yourself a chart and mark down every ounce of water that you drink. At the end of the day give yourself a score. I bet you drank more water today than you did yesterday. If so, give yourself a pat on the back, and keep working on your good health.

RESPECT FOR OTHERS

> "Treat all people alike. Give them all the same law. Give them all an even chance to live and grow … All people should have equal rights upon the earth."[9]

Be respectful to all, for example, treat everyone as a gentleman or lady, not necessarily because they are one, but because you are a gentleman or lady.

Another standard of civility is to respect others because all have a certain amount of worth–just because they are human. I like the old saying, "God doesn't make any junk." Everyone has worth in one area or another. We are not all the same. We have been raised by different parents, with different experiences, cultures, races, religions, philosophies, and customs. The richness of the many diverse backgrounds is very stimulating to the inquiring mind. Why not learn as much as possible about human nature and how we got to this point in history? "America is not like a blanket … America is more like a quilt—many patches, many pieces, many colors, many sizes, all woven together and held together by a common thread."[10]

It is our duty to treat everyone with respect, but this does not mean that we have to admire everyone or look up to them as role models. What it does mean is we should all

                                    MARJORIE BARCOMB

live by the Golden Rule: *Do unto others as you would have them do unto you*. It is interesting to note that all major religions and great philosophers ascribe to the Golden Rule in one form or another:

- Buddhism: Hurt not others with that which pains thyself.
- Christianity: Do unto others as you would have them do unto you.
- Judaism: What you dislike for yourself, do not do to anyone.
- Hinduism: Do nothing to thy neighbor which thou wouldst not have him do to thee thereafter.
- Islam: No one of you is a believer unless he loves for his brother what he loves for himself.
- Confucius: What you do not want done to yourself, do not do unto others.
- Aristotle: We should behave to others as we wish others to behave to us.[11]

I guess we could all agree that the Golden Rule is a universally accepted standard of good behavior. If everyone lived by the Golden Rule, what a wonderful world it would be.

Prejudice and discrimination, no matter what, are disrespectful when it comes to race, religion, stature, intelligence, etc. We cannot help what color we are, if we are born rich or poor, if we are Christian, Jewish, or any other religion, if we are short or tall, or if our IQ is 80 or 160. We still all deserve to be treated with respect, and it is our duty and responsibility to treat everyone else with respect.

When are we allowed to discriminate? When are we

allowed to be prejudiced? What do these words really mean?

Let's start with discrimination. Discrimination means being biased, showing favoritism, being intolerant, or to distinguish, to tell apart, to differentiate. As I said before, all other things being constant, we should never show discrimination when it comes to race, religion, stature, intelligence, etc. So when can we and must we discriminate? Coaches discriminate in selecting a team. I simply will not be chosen to be a NFL football player, and chances are you won't either. That is not equity, that's discrimination (distinguishing the good player from the not so good player). That is selection based on talent and skill. We think this is okay, but it is discrimination.

When are we allowed to be prejudiced? We all show prejudice in which sports events we like to participate in and observe, which foods we like to eat, etc. Part of life is picking and choosing based on qualifications, preference, merit, seniority, need, equity, effort, strength, intelligence, or skill. We end up with different degrees of fairness or unfairness depending on the situation. But we must all do our best to be as fair as possible.

We accept and show tolerance for the customs of people who were raised in a different culture; in fact, many of us embrace many of their traditions. I absolutely love to try new foods that traditionally come from various parts of the world. Studying the history of different cultures can be very enlightening. It can move us forward or prevent us from repeating some of their mistakes. All learning is beneficial.

Just as we want others to accept our customs and traditions, we should learn to accept others' customs and traditions as long as they are not illegal, immoral or unethical. I don't have to eat kidney pie, but I don't care if you do.

We should not be tolerant of immoral, disrespectful, or illegal behavior. The word tolerance seems to have been used mostly in its narrowest meaning. Generally, when we hear the word tolerance, it deals with race or cultural differences. There are many things that we should not tolerate. We should be intolerant with respect to child abuse, sexual deviancy, corruption, and any other immoral, hurtful, or illegal behaviors no matter the race, religion, or political bent of the perpetrator.

I definitely want my religion to be respected, and in following the Golden Rule, I must in good conscience respect the religions of others provided those religions do not disrespect our country or any of our laws, or perform any immoral function. It pains me greatly when I think of the number of people who have died in the name of religion; and it is still going on. Jihadists still want to kill anyone who does not ascribe to their religion. If we want our freedom of religion to remain intact, we must be willing to respect other law abiding and moral religions as well.

All people should be respected, no matter if their philosophy is liberal or conservative. I know many people who call themselves liberal who follow the rules and live by the universal standards of civility. I also know many people who are conservative who live by the same set of standards. Each has its own philosophical base.

I want you to remember that everyone has had different experiences and thus behave differently; we need to respect that. We cannot always put ourselves in someone else's moccasins, but we must try. When people seem to exhibit weird behavior, it may be that they are going through an extremely traumatic time in their life. They may be losing a loved one and can't understand why. They may be unemployed. They may be sick. There are thousands of reasons why someone might not behave exactly the way we think they ought to. That is no reason to be disrespectful.

Privacy is very important to most people, and we must respect that. We should never pry into anyone's affairs or eaves drop on their conversations. We should never just drop by anyone's home without being invited. When calling individuals on the phone, it is respectful to ask if they have a few minutes to talk. They may be the middle of a family dinner or be involved in some other activity and don't want to be interrupted. It is disrespectful to call late at night or early in the morning; you may be waking someone. When we exhibit this type of respect to our family, friends, and co-workers, we will be repaid considerably with the respect we will receive in return.

Others' careers, leisure time activities, and relationships are their business and none of ours. We should respect their choices in these matters. Again we must adhere to the Golden Rule. Would you want someone to choose your career, your leisure time activities, and your relationships? I'm sure the answer is, "No," so you have no reason to think about or comment on anyone else's.

Dressing appropriately for the occasion shows respect for others in the audience. Wearing skimpy or showy clothing to a business meeting or a family dinner is not appropriate and makes some people very uncomfortable. Likewise, we don't wear tuxedos to the beach. There is a time and place for various types of dress, and we should remember to respect others by dressing accordingly.

Good manners are another indicator of respect for others. People around you really appreciate a 'please,' 'thank you,' or 'excuse me.' I love to have someone open the door for me and by the same token, I enjoy opening the door for others. Chivalry is not dead!

A small reward for manners occurred when a flight attendant who was serving drinks on a recent flight approached my row; I asked, "May I have a Pepsi, please?" The flight attendant looked at me strangely, like she had not understood what I had said. I repeated the request, and she smiled broadly. Upon receiving my drink, I said, "Thank you." After serving everyone in the cabin their drinks, she returned to me and handed me two bags of peanuts and said, "You get these because you are the only person who thanked me for their beverage." Imagine that—a 737 loaded to capacity and no one thanked her. Now I was the one who was shocked! Just a little bit of manners goes a long way.

Manners make us civil, and they should be part of how we behave with family members, friends, co-workers, acquaintances, and even strangers. We should always show common courtesies such as making sure to RSVP when we are invited. If we all work together on using good manners and our belief that they are part of being civil to each other, we can make a real difference.

We drive carefully, and don't let our friends drive drunk

because we respect the safety of others; we help others who need a hand; we practice good manners even with strangers; we smile and let our light shine, not because we admire everyone, but because we respect others as individuals sharing our planet. It is simply the right thing to do. It is part of being human. It is part of being civil.

Refusing to listen to and to consider another's point of view is disrespectful. We should be tolerant of others' opinions, even when we disagree. We should disagree respectfully. Conversely, it is disrespectful to remain quiet when, if we offered constructive information, we could help someone get a job, get a promotion, or enhance their destiny.

Another extremely disrespectful and distasteful act is taking advantage of the underprivileged, whether it is the needy or the unenlightened. That's why I think it is so important for everyone to study, learn, and become as enlightened as possible. Lenin called the unenlightened useful idiots, and in their ignorance, they gave up their freedom. Hitler said, "What luck for rulers that men do not think."[12] Remember the keys to success and happiness are freedom and wisdom, and the wise are not led astray.

The list of disrespectful actions towards others is immense. Just a few more include gossip, hurtful allegations, forcing yourself ahead of someone who is in a line, not opening a door for an elderly or disabled person, using foul language and swearing, waking someone who really needs to sleep, belittling and screaming, taking more than your share, being grumpy, and negative. I'm sure you could add several other disrespectful actions to the ones we have already talked about.

A note of clarification—respect is not to be confused with fear. Those who are gang leaders demand respect from their members. Their members fear them–that isn't respect; that's intimidation.

Practice your self-talk, practice your mental imagery, and monitor your actions.

Every Day Say:

- I treat everyone as a gentleman or lady.
- I know everyone has worth in one area or another.
- I always follow the Golden Rule, no matter what.
- I know prejudice and discrimination are disrespectful when it comes to race, religion, stature, intelligence, and other human differences.
- I am tolerant of all that is legal, moral, and good.
- I am tolerant of cultural differences.
- I respect others' privacy.
- When I call someone, I always ask, "Do you have a minute?"
- I do not call anyone early in the morning or late at night unless it is an emergency.
- I respect others' choice of career.
- I respect others' choice of leisure activities.
- I respect others' choice of relationships.
- I am always courteous and use good manners.
- I do not interrupt others when they are speaking.
- I never take advantage of anyone.
- I listen intently when others are talking.
- I always consider another's point of view.

- I offer constructive information if I think it will help someone.

Practice makes perfect. So practice your self-talk until you automatically respond in concert with high principles.

One mental image that you can easily start practicing is picturing yourself calling someone, a friend, a co-worker, a client, your boss, or anyone else. See yourself saying, "Hi this is (your name). Do you have a minute?" By mentally practicing this routine or drill, your phone answering skills will improve immediately, and you will be showing respect for the other party's time.

If you choose the phone answering scenario, start jotting down every phone call you initiate, and score yourself on how many times you asked the respectful question, "Do you have a minute?" I'm sure that you will show improvement the first day after reading this section. Good job!

RESPECT FOR PROPERTY AND THE ENVIRONMENT

"The earth we abuse and the living things we kill will, in the end, take their revenge; for in exploiting their presence we are diminishing our future."[13]

Civilization is a way of living, and we all have to live here together. Let's keep our planet beautiful. Even though we live in the land of plenty, waste has become rampant. We have become a throw-away society. Now we're crushing good cars. We throw away a nice thick plastic bread bag and buy a thin skimpy sandwich bag. Our dishes are replaced with Styrofoam throw-away plates and containers.

 MARJORIE BARCOMB

Silverware is replaced with throw-away plastic-ware. Cloth towels are replaced with throw-away paper towels. I could cite many more examples of the things we think we need in our modern society. Things that we do not need at all are taxing our environment and our pocketbooks. It doesn't make any sense. (I am, however, thankful for bathroom tissue. I do remember the Sears catalogue.) Think about the things that you waste every day.

You must respect and maintain your property and your possessions. Many are buying new just to "keep up with the Joneses" or because the media deception has cast its bait, caught individuals when they were weak, and lured them in. Having a beautiful home, furniture, and possessions is a great privilege, and I salute those who have been successful and can afford what they have. But it is our duty to take care of what we have.

It is our responsibility to keep our home, our yard, and our neighborhood clean. If we respect ourselves, our neighbors, our community, and our environment, it is a privilege to do so.

It is our duty to respect what belongs to others, whether it is individually or collectively, both private and public. Many young individuals seem to think that it is okay to write on or destroy property that belongs to others, the school, or community. This frequently stems from lack of discipline on the part of their parents. These tagging behaviors demonstrate a total lack of respect for the property of others.

In respecting the environment we must be conservative about the use of natural resources. We should do our best to conserve energy. We need to keep our highways clean and free from litter. We need to keep our waterways clean and free from chemicals, debris, and sewage. Proper disposal of appliances, old cars, paint, chemicals, tires, etc. is also our responsibility. There are many recycling sites where you can dispose of these items. Some will even pay you for certain materials.

Respecting our rules and laws is another required and necessary element in maintaining a civil society. Some things are legal but they are not ethical. Just because something is legal doesn't necessarily mean it is the right thing to do. Bankruptcy is legal, but in some cases it is not ethical because it may have been preplanned to scam money from some source.

Appreciate and take care of everything that deserves care and respect. We all share this planet. Let's take care of it, and all that we have been blessed to own.

Practice your self-talk, practice your mental imagery, and monitor your actions.

Every Day Say:

- I do not waste my time.
- I do not waste natural resources.
- I do not waste my money.
- I respect and maintain my property and possessions.
- I respect the property and possessions of others.
- When I borrow something, I always return it clean and in good condition.
- When I rent something from a rental company, I treat it as though it were my own.

- I conserve energy to the best of my ability.
- I never litter our highways or countryside.
- I never pollute our waterways in any way.
- I re-cycle to the best of my ability.
- I appreciate all that I have and am thankful every day.

The state of our economy and our energy situation makes the aforementioned statements most profound. Not only should you repeat these statements for the specified time to make a difference in your life, it would be great if you shared them with others.

Hot water is a commodity that requires a lot of electricity. Picture yourself opening your electric bill and seeing quite a substantial decrease in what you owe because you have either turned off your hot water for several hours each day, or because you have turned down the temperature on your hot water tank. If you live in one of the warmer southern states, you can easily turn on your hot water for just a few hours each day. I know this works because I live in Arizona and I turn on my hot water for 30 to 40 minutes each morning, and even after two showers, I have hot to warm water for the rest of the day, as well as a substantial decrease in my electric bill. Every little thing that you do to decrease your energy consumption will make you feel good about what you are doing for the environment. A constructive spin-off is an increase in your fiscal responsibility.

Pay close attention to everything you do with respect to your property and possessions, to other's property and possessions, and to the environment. Document everything you do to improve in these areas. Evaluate your actions daily, and continue on your quest to improve in each of these areas. Always praise yourself for improvement.

RESPONSIBILITY MAKES YOU WORTHWHILE

*"We make guilty of our disasters
the sun, the moon, the stars, as
if we were villains on necessity,
fools by heavenly compulsion."[1]*

The effort put forth by people to excuse their irresponsibility is simply remarkable. Blame is placed on circumstances, on the alignment of the stars and planets, or any other celestial event deemed possible. This coupled with the learned helplessness, victimization, and perceived victimization believed by many in America are causing many economic problems that are driving our nation closer to the brink of collapse. This impending disaster can only be prevented through serious responsible behavior on the part of everyone, not just the worker bees. In *A Nation of Victims*, Charles Sykes states, "Increasingly, Americans act as if they received a lifelong indemnification from misfortune and a contractual release from personal responsibility."[2] We need to change this mindset. How unfortunate, for those who feel victimized. It is in continuing to feel victimized that prosperity for them will never occur. They will remain in their little box that I call the 'learned helplessness box' and become targets for exploitation.

If you feel that you are a victim of birth or circumstances, now is the time to get busy and change the vicious cycle in which you feel trapped. I know; I've been there!

Take advantage of the freedom offered by our Constitution and make sure that these freedoms are not taken away or you will definitely stay in your box forever. Keep in mind that no nation has been so blessed and so free as the U. S. in all of history. By following the precepts laid down in this book you are off to a flying start. You are the only one who can make a difference in your life. If you continuing doing what you are now doing, you will get the same result. If you want a different result, then you must change how you think and what you do.

Responsible people take full responsibility for themselves and their actions; they do not blame others for their shortcomings or point fingers at others for their mistakes. They embody many characteristics that make them successful and productive members of society. A major spin-off is happiness. Most of what happens in your life boils down to 'you reap what you sow.'

There are many facets of being a responsible person, and I know you want to be an ace in this area. As in any other of the universal standards, no matter where you stand, responsibility can be learned and/or improved upon. You will find that responsibility encompasses many of the concepts that we have already talked about.

As you read through this chapter you may feel that you are indeed responsible, and if that is the case, use what you have read to help others. Every phrase, every sentence, every conversation that helps people become more responsible is priceless. Changing lives for the better is always a worthy enterprise.

We must accept the consequences of all our actions.

When making poor decisions, responsible individuals accept the consequences and learn from them. These are the lessons of life. We don't make excuses, ignore the results, or blame others. When making good sound decisions, we profit from them and try to prevent others from falling into a trap. That's being accountable. When making decisions, you will always find it responsible and profitable to think long-term rather than making snap decisions without thinking through all the possible consequences. In looking at the big picture, when making decisions, ask yourself, "What are the consequences now, tomorrow, later on; to the people I love, to my finances, on myself, on my degree of stress, on society, on any and all stakeholders?" To emphasize this point consider the thirty year mortgage scenario and answer each of these questions when comparing the thirty year mortgage to the three seven year mortgages. Which do you think has the least hurtful consequences? Which do you think exhibits the greatest degree of responsible character? It is our duty to become as responsible as we can.

Responsible people feel the sense of duty with respect to their fellowman, country, family, job, and themselves. To be responsible you must obey the laws and rules governing your country, state, and community, provided they are not immoral. If you are male, you must display loyalty to your country by registering for military service when you reach eighteen years of age. You must pay your fair share of taxes, both local and federal.

It is also your duty to pay your bills and/or live up to any other promissory notes or promises in which you have either given your word or signed a contract. The only way responsible people can get out of these is if they become seriously ill, and there is just no human way possible for them to live up to their promises that were originally made in good faith.

It is your duty to become a productive member of society; that is, you must have a job. As part of your job, it is your responsibility to be punctual, loyal to your employer and put forth the effort required to produce excellent results. You should take pride in workmanship. In looking at the works of Michelangelo, the fine paintings, etc., I ask myself, *where has this kind of pride gone?* It seems the rule of the day is to just do enough to get by; problems with the economy?–No wonder! Just getting by is not responsible behavior. When hired by an employer, there is either an unwritten or written contract that you will commit to doing the job, and in turn you will have a specific monetary gain, a paycheck. You must do what is expected–it is your job. "You must work and do well; not be lazy…if you wish to earn happiness. Laziness may appear attractive, but work gives satisfaction."[3] You must be committed to your job. Commitment means you will do what you said you will do.

You may feel that the job you are doing is beneath you, that the work requires simple tasks. Small tasks are just as important as bigger tasks because they are part of the complete picture. In the words of Helen Keller, "I long to accomplish a great and noble task, but it is my chief duty to accomplish small tasks as if they were great and noble."[4] All work is meaningful and self-discipline is a badge of honor.

You do not necessarily have to work for someone else

                                           MARJORIE BARCOMB

to be a productive member of society. The entrepreneurial spirit is alive and well. By being both educated and wise, you may very well start your own business or tap into your God given talents and skills to earn a substantial living and help others at the same time. Private enterprise can provide for motivation and advancement, not only for the individual ownership but for the spin offs coming from their research.

Another responsibility tied to your employment is that you provide the effort necessary to complete your job effectively. Efficiency = effectiveness /effort. To explain this ratio, when you develop a process that is very effective and requires little effort, the efficiency is high. When the effectiveness is minimal and much effort is needed, the efficiency is low. As you become more and more responsible, it is valuable to look at how effective your efforts are. This will be a guide as you determine whether to continue using the same processes or to try a different approach. Don't be impatient; just keep trying. "Desire to have things done quickly prevents their being done thoroughly."[5]

Another source of duty comes into play when looking at our duties as a parent, child, employer, employee, friend, acquaintance, etc. You can readily see that your duty as a parent or your duty as an employee is much greater than your duty toward an acquaintance whom you merely need to respect. A major duty as a parent is to teach your children the universal standards of civility that they should live by, and you have a great start just by reading this book. Children have the duty and obligation to obey their parents in all that is legal and moral. It is everyone's duty to live by the ethical principles laid out in the universal standards of civility. In the words of Marie Curie,

> You cannot hope to build a better world without improving the individuals. To that end each of us must work for our own improvement and at the same time share a general responsibility for all humanity, our particular duty being to aid those to whom we think we can be most useful.[6]

It is your responsibility to take care of your own life. It is your responsibility to be in control of every aspect of your life, such as controlling your anger, your temper, your words, your eating habits, your health habits, your exercise, your emotions, your desires and appetites, your goals, your time, and your money. It is your choice as to whether or not you want to be responsible, but it will affect your life. It may do so in a big way. "Destiny is not a matter of chance, it is a matter of choice, it is not a thing to be waited for; it is a thing to be achieved."[7]

Practice your self-talk, practice your mental imagery, and monitor your actions.

Every Day Say:

- I am not a victim.
- I create my own circumstances.
- I love being busy.
- I am not lazy.
- I take full responsibility for my actions and my life.
- I learn from my mistakes.
- I think 'out of the box'.
- I enjoy being responsible.

- I gain in wisdom every day.
- I appreciate my freedom.
- I think before I act.
- I do not jump to conclusions without all the facts.
- I do not blame others or circumstances for my mistakes.
- I am dependable.
- It is my duty to be loyal to my country in all that is not immoral.
- It is my duty to be loyal to my family in all that is not immoral.
- I obey the laws.
- I pay my fair share of taxes.
- I pay my bills.
- I keep my promises.
- I honor all my contracts, both oral and written.
- I am a productive member of society.
- I am loyal to my employer.
- I am always on time.
- I pursue excellence in everything I do.
- I take pride in my work.
- I always go the extra mile.
- I do menial tasks with a good heart.
- I believe in entrepreneurship.
- I nurture and practice my skills and talents.
- I give one hundred percent.
- I do not give up until the job is completed.
- I honor my parents.
- I teach my children the universal standards of civility.

- I treat everyone with respect.
- I listen to the ideas of others.
- I always practice self control.
- My destiny depends on me and me alone.
- I live by the ethical principles laid out in the universal standards of civility.
- My life has a purpose, and that is to make this world a better place.

You can see that there is a lot of overlap with other standards of civility when we talk about responsibility. Prioritize the self-talk statements, and work on your highest priority ones first.

Because responsibility is such an all encompassing standard, you could come up with not just dozens but hundreds of mental pictures to store in your arsenal of visualizations that you want to become your reality. Picture yourself completing a task; it could be redecorating a room, remodeling your house, writing a paper, preparing a presentation, or even a menial task. See yourself pursuing excellence and perfection in your work. Really feel the feeling of pride in a job well done.

Using the list of responsibility self-talk statements, focus on your actions each day. In the evening look at the list, and examine what you have done during the day. Where do you see improvement? What can you do tomorrow to improve further? Again, any improvement is worthy of note. Persevere!

LOYALTY AND FAITHFULNESS PROVIDE YOU LOVE AND SECURITY

"The person who commands well must have obeyed others in the past, and the person who obeys well is worthy of being someday a commander."[1]

When I think of loyalty I think of dogs. Dogs love you no matter what. You can come home grumpy, sweaty, and negative, and they are always glad to see you and show you love. Wouldn't it be nice if everyone was like this? Even your most private secrets are safe with your pooch. Your dog looks past his or her needs and is your loyal friend. We need to think the same way. It is important and fulfilling to look out for people who love and care for you. We should always pledge our loyalty to, stand up for, and protect, our family, our friends, our employment, and our country.

When we pledge loyalty to our family, we provide for their needs by putting them first. We spend time with them. With family it is easy to be loyal. It's called love.

We demonstrate fidelity to our spouse by keeping our vows and including him/her in all major family decisions. It is important to continue to treat our spouse as we did when we were dating. Frequently married people fall into the trap of getting in a rut, feeling that they could have chosen more wisely, and start to entertain repetitive destructive thoughts both for themselves and for their marriage. Think positive. For example, if your spouse leaves a pair of shoes in the middle of the family room, think, "A good man/woman wears those shoes," not "I wish the 'slob' would pick up after himself/herself." When the glitz of being a newlywed starts to wear off, it's amazing how little things like 'shoes' can start a chain of thoughts that are ultimately destructive to the relationship. Instead make a joke about those dog-gone shoes. Your family room will be there long after you are gone. Only the most cherished memories of loved ones remain. Your spouse and your children should be cherished and your highest priority.

Your children deserve good direction and it is your duty to provide it. I chose a career as a teacher, although that would not have normally been my first choice, but I wanted to be home with my children when they were not in school. Their safety, security and upbringing were high on my list of priorities. That choice turned out to be the biggest reward of my life. I have three wonderful, principled, and successful sons. Now, I look at teaching as a lesson in my own personal development and a stepping stone to fulfilling my dreams.

We are loyal to our friends when we want what is best for their well-being. You've heard the expression, "Friends don't let friends drive drunk." This is just one example of being loyal to our friends. We should protect our friends and offer constructive service. True and good friends do not ask you to participate in any action that is hurtful, unhealthy, or illegal. Those who do are not friends; they are people who need someone else to share in their vices to make them feel better about themselves. They are only thinking of themselves. They are selfish and need professional help. If you feel that you need these people as friends, *you* have a problem. You are needy. To improve your life, you must passionately and diligently dive into working on your self-esteem. Remember, loyalty should only be exercised in all that is moral and good. Otherwise, you are not being loyal; you are being an enabler. "Some people don't want you to make it because they're not going to make it … Don't give up! Surround yourself with people who are energetic and disciplined."[2]

Another facet of being loyal is controlling your tongue. Don't gossip—keep things to yourself unless it is praise for others. Gossip can cut like a sword and torment like a fatal illness. Most importantly, gossip serves no useful purpose in the family, in friendships or at work. It may seem difficult to control the tongue at first, but with practice it is amazing how much you can control what you say. Remember, talking about someone else's dilemma does not lighten your burden or raise your status. "The only way to have a friend is to be one."[3]

Loyalty and faithfulness are twin concepts. Close, lasting relationships hinge on faithfulness. A faithful person is always there when needed and never betrays a trust or commitment. Loyalty and faithfulness allow those around us to be comfortable in their relationship with us. There is no stress, deceit, or distrust. Everyone deserves to have friends and relationships with loyal, trusting, faithful people. Let it start with you.

Even being loyal to a boss or co-worker that is tough

on you helps you to grow in tolerance and in the understanding of human nature. You may not have this boss or co-worker all your life, but what you learn will illuminate your path when you rise to a position of authority. You will not be repeating his or her mistakes. You will be a better person for what you have learned. "He who is to be a good ruler must have first been ruled."[4]

Finally, we pledge our loyalty to our country by saying the "Pledge of Allegiance to the Flag." But how many people truly know what they are pledging? You need to know something about what you are pledging your allegiance to. It is our duty to learn about our Republic. It is our duty to learn about the historical documents produced by our Founding Fathers. These documents are crucial to whom we are as a people and as a nation. The Articles of Confederation, the Constitution, (especially the Preamble), the Bill of Rights, the Declaration of Independence, and the Gettysburg Address are all part of our history as a nation. Not only should we understand these documents, but we should also know the history behind them, and the biographies of their signers. Correct education into our real history will prevent us from being blind-sided by media spin and political propaganda. Not everyone in government is a person of high moral fiber, so we must be ever so vigilant.

The lack of civic knowledge is alarming. The *Yuma Sun,* in an article by Mike Shelton, in the summer of 2009, reported survey results of 2,508 Americans who took a civics test from Intercollegiate Studies Institute.[5] The vast majority did not know that "government of the people, by the people, and for the people, shall not perish from the Earth" came from Lincoln's Gettysburg Address. Even more alarming, he stated, the following statistics:

- Seventy-nine percent of those who had been elected to government office did not know the Bill of Rights expressly prohibits establishing an official religion for the U.S.
- Thirty percent did not know that "life, liberty, and the pursuit of happiness" are inalienable rights referred to in the Declaration of Independence.
- Twenty-seven percent could not name even one right or freedom guaranteed by the First Amendment.
- Forty-three percent did not know what the Electoral College does. One in five thought it either "trains those aspiring for higher political office" or "was established to supervise the first televised presidential debates.
- Fifty-four percent did not know the Constitution gives Congress the power to declare war.

Shelton gave many more examples, but I think with the examples given that you can readily discern that we are indeed a nation in crisis. What seems to be getting lost in our nation today is the development of good character and an understanding of our true history. The development of good character by the incorporation of universal standards or values that have stood the test of time in every facet of our lives should be deliberately and proactively taught by parents, schools, community organizations, and churches.

Accurate historical accounts and founding documents should also be taught and cherished.

Loyalty to family, friends, co-workers, bosses, and country provide the continued safety and security that we cherish. It is to our personal benefit that we nurture all these factors in our lives.

Practice your self-talk, practice your mental imagery, and monitor your actions.

Every Day Say:

- I look out for my family.
- I look out for my friends.
- I always keep secrets.
- I never gossip.
- I think before I talk.
- I value my relationships; therefore, I am loyal.
- I am always loyal to my employer.
- I am loyal to my country.
- I study my nation's history.
- I study my nation's founding documents.
- I read about my nation's founding fathers.
- I read, I study, and I come to my own conclusions.

Remember the Rule of Thirty Days.

There are many examples where you could practice mental images dealing with loyalty. In fact, you can come up with several examples dealing with each of the above self-talk statements. Prioritize the list then pick one or two that you would like to work on first.

Let's assume all the girls in the office have a bad habit of gossiping during the lunch hour and you have just decided that you do not want to be part of this destructive enterprise any longer. Picture yourself walking away and doing something constructive. There are many constructive things you could see in your mind's eye. Maybe you could see yourself writing a thank you note to someone just for being a nice person, or maybe you can picture yourself at your computer looking up information about our nation's founding documents. Whatever you see yourself doing make sure that loyalty is the theme of your imagery.

Start to monitor your actions with respect to the self-talk stated above. Each evening as you assess your actions for the day, what progress are you seeing? Every little nanosecond of improvement is valuable. Never give up, and always give yourself the credit you richly deserve for your progress.

SERVICE PROVIDES INTRINSIC REWARDS AND INCREASES YOUR SELF-WORTH

"When you cease to make a contribution, you begin to die."[1]

One way that we demonstrate loyalty is through service. Service, to me, means serving for the right reasons. I find that some people perform community service so that it will look good on a resume or to get into college. People who engage in this behavior are only fooling themselves. My advice is to continue doing community service anyway because the intrinsic rewards gained are more than worth the effort. Hopefully, some of these individuals will start to enjoy the intrinsic rewards gained and begin to do community service for the right reasons.

How can you perform community service? Most people donate their time, but you can also donate money and/or your expertise. Some people donate their entire careers to serve and protect their fellow countrymen.

When thinking about service to others, you might start close to home and then expand your horizons. You can begin by asking yourself, "What can I do to help my family and others that live in my neighborhood?" Much can be done on the local level because needs exist everywhere. A few things that you might consider include the following: serving on boards, volunteering at the hospital, visiting nursing home residents, visiting the sick, reading to the infirm, delivering food to the home-bound, reading to children, teaching children to read, providing transportation for the elderly, ill and/or disabled, and cleaning the neighborhood.

You can help in protecting our environment by recycling metals, paper, glass, and plastic, as well as disposing of appliances, tires, batteries, chemicals, and other environmentally unfriendly materials in an appropriate manner. Most communities have depositories for potentially harmful scrap.

You can serve your community by participating in the political process. Attendance and participation in town-hall meetings is a great way for you to state your opinion and to have your voice heard. This may seem a bit difficult at first, but it really is your duty to let your legislators know the feelings of his or her constituents.

Serving as members of the town, county, state, or federal boards or legislatures also provides service, although these do not always constitute altruistic participation. Many serve for self-gratifying motives. This does not amount to service; it amounts to personal advantage. Thankfully there are individuals who do serve for the sole purpose of representing their constituents, and that is true service whether they are paid or not.

Other boards, such as school boards, hospital boards, foundation boards, and college boards generally are non-paying positions, and the service provided by these board members is often times more selfless. The intrinsic reward, valued by such participation, is all the pay that many of these trustees seek.

		

Service to our community and our country also means being a good citizen. You serve your community and country by studying the issues facing your community and our nation so you can vote intelligently. If you have not read and learned about the issues, consult someone whom you trust to explain them to you. Diligently search for and make use of many sources to gather information. Depending on just one source may give you a very biased perspective. This could be counter-productive to the future of your community and our nation. If, in the end, you feel that you don't understand what's going on–don't vote. You could be making a mistake. Remember, people rallied behind Adolph Hitler! They thought he was charismatic, and they believed everything he said. If it sounds too good to be true, it probably is.

One of your goals could be to donate a specific number of hours each week or each month to community service. If you don't make community service one of your written goals, you probably will never get around to it. That would be a loss for both you and your community.

To be of service to our community and fellow man, we must follow the rules and the laws, provided they are not immoral. Some things are legal but are not necessarily moral. As I said before, bankruptcy is legal, but it is immoral if a person intentionally runs up credit cards for the sole purpose of filing for bankruptcy. In this life nothing is free; someone has to pay the price. Other borrowers have to pay higher interest rates to make up for what the credit card company lost through the bankruptcy. Understand that the bankruptcy law was put in place originally as a safety-net to help people who had good intentions and the means to pay for their bills; but they either became ill or unemployed through no fault of their own making them unable to fulfill their obligation.

The next way to do service is to donate money. Homeless shelters, missions, churches, college scholarship foundations, 'back to school supplies' programs, and medical research are some entities that desperately need a helping hand. Never feel that your donation is too small to make a difference. One dollar from a million people has the same effect as a million dollars from one person. A lot of little donations may add up to a cure for a devastating disease or may be used for some other human benefit.

The last way you can do service is to donate your expertise. Many individuals write columns in the paper where they provide information in their chosen field of education or interest. Some people do spots on the local radio and/or TV programs by sharing their knowledge in various areas of interest common to the listening audience. Sharing constructive and beneficial information is a very worthy cause and profits everyone. Wouldn't it be nice to say, "I'm doing what I think I was put on this earth to do. And I'm really grateful to have something that I'm passionate about and that I think is profoundly important."[2]

Another area of expertise where individuals are trained and educated to provide their service to our country is the military. They serve by educating themselves with the issues and face their adversaries with loyalty and courage. They care about the direction the country is going and the welfare and security of all its citizens. One of the most

                    MARJORIE BARCOMB

basic human needs is security. Because of their service, we as a nation have been relatively secure for many years. This results from the sacrifice and selfless service provided by our brave men and women.

Whether you provide service by studying the issues, donating your time, donating your money, or providing your expertise, all that you do for others enriches your life, enhances your character, and develops your community and our country. It becomes a better place to live because of you. You leave your mark.

Practice your self-talk, practice your mental imagery, and monitor your actions.

- I serve on an in-kind board at …
- I volunteer at the …
- I visit the …
- I read to the …
- I teach …
- I provide transportation for the …
- I pick up trash and keep my neighborhood clean.
- I recycle.
- I dispose of items correctly.
- I participate in the political process.
- I attend meetings that affect my country's future.
- I vote for issues only when I understand them.
- I vote for candidates only when I have studied their voting records.
- I study the issues facing our nation and its future.
- I serve in the military.
- I donate _____ hours to community service each month.

- I obey all the rules and laws provided they are not immoral.
- I donate money to…
- I donate my expertise to…
- I write a column in the…
- I do spots on the local radio to…

Certainly, you cannot do all the above self-talk ideas. Pick the one(s) you feel that you could do and do well. Every little bit helps. Once you have selected your self-talk statement(s), make sure you start your thirty day regimen.

Picture yourself delivering food to an elderly couple who can no longer leave their home. As you walk in the door, their pooch greets you with brisk tail wags. He knows why you are there. The elderly couple smile softly and exude love and thankfulness. Your heart is filled with compassion as your mind wanders to your own aging parents. Your mind continues to wander as you then put yourself in their shoes. You come back to earth when the tail wagging pooch licks your hand. Now you are the one who is thankful. You give them a hug and retreat to your vehicle. Your chest is bursting with emotion—all is well!

As you select from the self-talk list, prepare a plan wherein you can help others. Even a few minutes a day or a couple hours each week from many individuals really make a tremendous difference to one in need. Monitor your actions, and evaluate your success as you become an altruistic person with high principles. Your self-worth just took a major leap upward!

FAIRNESS, CARING, AND THANKFULNESS EARN YOU RESPECT

"We may never know the good a simple smile can do. May no one ever come to you without going away better and happier. May everyone see kindness in your face, in your eyes, in your smile… Love is a fruit in season at all times."[1]

What mental imagery do you evoke when you think of a fair and caring individual? Do you see someone who is kind, helpful, soft-spoken, giving, compassionate, and/or considerate? Is that person impartial and even-handed? Do they exhibit a thankful nature? All these adjectives describe a very special person, one that we all should seek to emulate. Notice how these adjectives are also inextricably tied to the universal standards that we have already talked about.

FAIRNESS

"We hold these truths to be self-evident: that all men are created equal."[2]

Fairness means being unbiased, even handed, scrupulous, open, and impartial. It also means that one who is fair is free from self-interest, prejudice, and/or favoritism. This is a difficult concept to get your arms around because sometimes situations and circumstances make it very difficult and time consuming to come to a fair and just decision. This is probably the toughest of all the universal standards to live by.

Recently, equity and equality seem to have become the buzz words when dealing with fairness. You hear people and/or organizations state that they make all their decisions based on equity and/or equality. Although equity and equality play a major role, frequently other unique considerations must come into play when dealing with fairness. It is important however, that all other aspects of fairness being equal, nothing takes the place of equality or equity. Here are a few examples where other fairness factors come into play.

At a boxing match the combination of strength, endurance, and talent determines the winner. The winner is also quite possibly the person who puts forth the most effort in training to prepare for the fight. Equity or equality doesn't seem to play a significant role here. Might is right.

In the selection of a college basketball team, what we consider fairness boils down to the best players being selected for the team. We don't even consider other aspects of fairness like seniority, merit, effort, equity or equality. There are many instances where unique aspects of fairness must come into play.

Talent is frequently considered a unique aspect of fairness. Is it fair that movie stars, top vocalists, and sports figures make salaries in the tens of millions while the median salary for hard working folks is in the thousands? Is this equity or equality? Is it based on need or seniority? Or is it simply because of the demand for their talent?

In looking at how various facets of fairness come into play, let's assume an employer is forced to cut back on the sales force because of a failing economy. The two newest employees are the best salesman. Is it fair to keep them when some older employees have been loyal to the company for several years and one is a single mom with children? As you can see determining fairness can sometimes be a daunting experience; many factors need intense scrutiny—seniority, need, loyalty, performance, effort, ability, creativity, strength, equity, talent, need, and so on. Sometimes it boils down to making sure what we decide will cause the minimal amount of hurt for all stakeholders.

You can't make snap decisions when it comes to fairness. It is crucial that all factors that impinge on your decision are weighed with care so that you can stand by and defend your decision with a rational defense at a later date. If you really care, you will spend the necessary time on decisions that deal with fairness. Caring individuals are compassionate, and they take all extenuating factors and circumstances into consideration when making decisions dealing with fairness. They look at the long-term ramifications.

CARING

"Always do these things: Show mercy to others; be kind, gentle, and patient." [3]

Showing concern for the survival and well-being of others is a demonstration of caring and compassion. Being sympathetic towards another's distress with the desire to alleviate it is another definition of compassion as defined by Webster's dictionary.

Caring individuals also show compassion towards people and animals who suffer pain, and they try to help alleviate suffering in any and every way possible. They show love and mercy towards those who are less fortunate. They know how to put themselves in someone else's shoes. They feel their pain. Caring people express a kind and gentle nature that is a shining star in the arsenal of their personal virtues.

THANKFULNESS

> "Gratitude expresses itself in a sincere thank you … not for the gifts of this day only, but for the day itself; not for what we believe will be ours in the future, but for the bounty of the past." [4]

Pain, distress, and suffering are part of the human condition which eventually affects us all, but how we deal with it determines the strength and depth of our character. I have found that when going through the storms of life, it is very helpful to write in a thankfulness journal each day. I suggest you do this every day even when things are going great! It is always uplifting to think about the things for which we should give thanks. When we write down all the things for which we are thankful, it's incredible to observe the number of items on our list, items that we normally take for granted. "Gratitude is the memory of the heart." [5]

Comparing your life to the lives of most people who inhabit this planet, I think you not only could be, but should be, very thankful. "If you have never experienced a war, an imprisonment, torture, or a famine, you are happier than 500 million people in this world."[6] "If there is a meal in your fridge, you are dressed and have shoes, you have a bed and a roof, you are better off than seventy five percent of the people in this world."[7] Do you have the freedom to choose in many areas of your life? Most people do not. The message is—give thanks.

Let us give thanks for living in a relatively free country, food on the table, a bed to sleep in, a roof over our head, the beautiful sunsets, the serene ponds and lakes, the fields of grain, the fruited plains, the flowers, the morning dew, the rain, the sunshine … I could go on for days stating all the blessings for which we should be thankful. Self-pity is a pity! Don't let society con you into believing that you need everything they are selling, whether material or philosophical. Stop the 'me' in all that you do. Pray for others, don't prey on others. You will overflow with joy as soon as you take the focus off yourself!

Practice your self-talk, practice your mental imagery, and monitor your actions.

- I think through all the facets of fairness before I make a decision.
- I take the time to make sure my decisions are fair.
- I help others who are in need.
- I pray for others.
- I am sympathetic when I see hurt or pain.
- I show compassion towards those who have been hurt in any way.
- I am thankful each day.
- I make a list of all the things I am thankful for.

- I read and write in my Thankfulness Journal each day.
- I always lend a helping hand to those who need it.

Select the self-talk statements that you want to work on as you build your character. You may choose to add some statements of your own.

Picture yourself as having lost your job. What are you feeling? Now continue your daydream to where you see yourself writing in your thankfulness journal. Because of your situation, you are making an extensive list all the things that you are and should be thankful for. Preparing this mental list takes several minutes. How do you feel now? You definitely have more hope for the future when you can be thankful for the past. It is easier to look for a new job and to get hired when you have a spring in your step and a smile on your face rather than an ambling walk and a frown.

Monitor everything you do each day, and evaluate yourself in the evening. Ask yourself, "What did I do today that showed how much I cared, how fair I was, and how thankful I was?" Remember, people don't care how much you know until they know how much you care. Praise yourself for paying close attention to your actions and ask yourself, "What can I do to improve tomorrow? Is there anything I could have done differently that would have had a greater impact on someone in need?"

A DECISION-MAKING MODEL THAT HELPS YOU MAKE DEFENSIBLE, RATIONAL DECISIONS WITH A CLEAR CONSCIENCE

"It's not hard to make decisions when you know what your values are."[1]

Your convictions determine your decision-making ability. Strong unbending convictions, based on the standards of civility, once internalized, will assist you in making strong, defensible decisions. The decisions that you make are determined by whether you are more interested in your character or in your reputation. They will demonstrate who you really are—on the inside.

Most people live with a matter of preference rather than being anchored in the values garnered from learning and from living by the timeless standards of integrity, forgiveness, respect, responsibility, loyalty, service, and fairness. Once you have internalized these standards, they will become part of your belief system. Your beliefs eventually become your convictions, and your convictions are precursors of your decision-making. Being convicted to the absolute truth of these timeless standards helps you make defensible, rational decisions, and to do so with a clear conscience.

The decisions you collectively make will determine the survival, not only of yourself and your family, but of our society, and of our nation. Once you compromise a small step in the wrong direction, you are opening yourself up to being led down a crooked path. A small misstep tolerated leads to a larger misstep, and little by little your values and convictions become eroded and corrupted. The convictions that you have that you will not compromise determine your degree of moral fortitude; however, this does not exempt you from the storms of life.

Life will test you, but a person of character will stand firm in his or her moral convictions, no matter what. Sometimes we can't understand. We ask, "Why is this happening to me or my family?" Even though some life circumstances can be very painful in the short-term, the long-term reward of having the moral courage to stand by our convictions is definitely worth the effort. It is better to ask ourselves, "What was I supposed to learn from that, and how can I become a better person because of it? How can I help others because of what I have learned?"

Wherever you go and whatever you do, take your convictions with you. Take your convictions with you to your school, to your work, to places of business, to the polls, and to your doctor. Live by your convictions when at home and with your family. Your convictions lead to your decision-making, and that determines your character. Remember, your character is who you really are when no one is looking.

Even though your reputation should be guarded, your character should always supersede your reputation. Your conscience that is developed from internalizing standards of civility should dictate that.

When making decisions it is important to make sure

　　　　　　　　　　　　　　　　MARJORIE BARCOMB

the facts used in making the decision are correct. We must be vigilant about our sources of information and make sure what we find is not tainted. We need to make sure our sources are living by the Golden Rule—that what they want for others is exactly what they want for themselves. Our sources of information must come from highly principled people otherwise our decisions may be faulty.

What questions should we ask ourselves as we are faced with a decision-making situation?

- Am I being a person of integrity, a person who is honest and truthful, trustworthy, reliable, and keeps my promises if my decision is to…?
- Am I a person who is willing to forgive if my decision is to…?
- Am I being respectful to myself, to others and to everything in my environment if my decision is to…?
- Am I being responsible, paying attention to duty, and being accountable for my actions if my decision is to…?
- Am I being loyal if my decision is to…?
- Am I providing the service to others that I should provide if my decision is to…?
- Am I being fair, based on seniority, need, loyalty, performance, effort, ability, creativity, strength, equity, talent, merit, gender, race, and/or equality depending on the situation if my decision is to…?

This may require concentrated thought.

You may think this is an exhausting system for making decisions, but it is crucial if you are a highly principled person. The best part is that you have come to your conclusions and your decisions by applying a rational test, and now you can make rational defensible arguments with respect to your position.

I use the mnemonic—*In forgiv*ing *r*owdy *r*ascals, *love* senses *fairness*. The italicized section of each word is my clue as to the standard I need to address.

- *In*—integrity
- *Forgiv*ing—forgiveness
- *R*owdy—respect
- *R*ascals—responsibility
- *Love*—loyalty
- *S*enses—service
- *Fairness*—fairness

Create your own mnemonic, and make it personal and easy to remember.

When you are asked questions such as, "Do you believe in capital punishment?" "Do you believe in abortion?" "Will you participate in a Ponzi scheme?" "Will you donate two hours per week to read to homeless children?" Please, remember your decisions are not your values but your value-judgments based on your convictions with respect to your values. When faced with making a decision, ask yourself, "Am I exhibiting integrity, forgiveness, respect, responsibility, loyalty, service, and/or fairness if my decision is to…?" If you ask yourself the seven questions listed above, you will be able to defend your answer and do so with clarity. When you use an iron-clad decision-making model based on standards of civility in all your decisions, people will come to trust you because they know that you do not flip-flop or waiver in your reasoning. You will be that highly principled person so many seek to emulate.

We are judged by the decisions we make, and how well we can defend our position with respect to those decisions. We tend to judge ourselves by the best things we have done and want others to judge us using the same template. Unfortunately, others judge us by the last worst thing we have done. You can tell the truth all your life, then slip up and tell one lie, and get caught. You are now considered a liar. This may not be a fair evaluation of your overall character, but it is now part of your reputation. That is why I say guard your reputation. "Character builds slowly, but [your reputation] can be torn down within incredible swiftness."[2]

A lot of people think that it is okay to do something unethical as long as everyone else is doing it. They say things like, "This is the 21st century." Unethical behavior, immorality, or lack of values is detrimental to all of us, no matter what century we are in. Anything that runs counter to the universal standards of civility is self-defeating. Bear in mind, good character is characterized not by what you say, but by what you do. Make sure your actions match your rhetoric.

When we face an ethical problem or dilemma, we generally are pretty sure what decision we should make with respect to the solution. Having the courage to do the right thing is another story. There are times when doing the right thing costs more than we are willing to pay. When we see the situation in that light, we are being cowards. We need to be careful not to underestimate the cost of doing the wrong thing. The cost of doing the wrong thing may bring to bear much more than we had assumed. Often, this is the case when people in authority put undue pressure on you for immediate results. It is wrong to meet deadlines to please someone in authority when you have not thought through the strategy to solve the problem or complete the program or project correctly and efficiently. The long-term consequences or effects could be catastrophic.

We live in an extremely uncertain time; therefore, we should be very vigilant with respect to decisions that will affect our lives and maybe even our children's and grandchildren's lives for many years to come. The well-being of our country, our lives, and our children's lives is determined by our good moral character. It is our duty and responsibility to study and understand the issues and to be involved in moral decision-making that not only affects us but our posterity. You must always promote what is right over what is expedient! We are role models whether we like it or not.

Practice your self-talk, practice your mental imagery, and monitor your actions.

Every Day Say:

- I do not make knee-jerk decisions.
- I do not jump to conclusions.
- I think about my character more than my reputation when I make decisions.
- I ask myself questions about the standards of civility when I make decisions.
- I ask myself if my decision demonstrates integrity.
- I ask myself if I must take forgiveness into consideration in making decisions.

- I ask myself if I am demonstrating fairness to all in my decisions.
- I make sure I am being responsible when I answer a question or make a decision with respect to an issue.
- My decisions always exhibit loyalty to my family, friends, church, community, and country.
- I am fair and caring in all my decisions.
- I make sure I can defend my decisions rationally and with a clear conscience.
- I have the moral fortitude to make hard decisions.

Now picture your seventeen year-old son asking you to sign for him to join the military. Will you make a knee-jerk decision, or will you take your time to come up with a rational and defensible decision? What questions are you going to ask him? What information will you need to collect before you make the decision? Your imagery should include you going through all the universal standards of civility before you finally decide what to do. Take your time as you go through each of these standards. Does your ultimate decision resemble your knee-jerk decision?

Evaluate the decisions that you make for the next few days. Do you see any improvement in how you implement your decision making process? If so, you are doing a great service for yourself, and you are helping others who are the recipients of the effects of your decisions.

PART 2

WHO ARE YOU?

WHO I AM

There are two reasons why I want to share a few of my life's struggles with you: first, so that you can identify in some way with the obstacles that I faced, and second, to show you how the steps I had to take in my battle to overcome and live a happier and more successful life led to *The Formula*. You too, can apply *The Formula* to your life. It will show you how to rise above your present circumstances and to take you to where you want to go. Where you've been is not important; it's where you are going that is important!

Just before I was born, my parents, with four children, were still reeling from the effects of the "Great Depression." They were extremely poor. This led them to make decisions that they otherwise probably would not have made. A major spin-off of one of their decisions affected my life in overwhelming ways. This led to bad dreams dominating my early life; I dreamed continually of monsters trying to kill me and other life threatening situations.

One dream in particular haunted me for the first fourteen years of my life. In this dream I was on a ship, and we were in a violent storm. I was alone. I was trying to hold on to the rail, but it was slippery and slimy. I was trying not to fall off the ship, but I knew that if I did, I would go to heaven. Then I heard a loud voice, as if from the sky above that said firmly, "We must turn the ship around." When the ship veered quickly around to the left, I nearly fell off, but I managed to hang on. The waters quieted, and we finally came to shore. My mom and dad were there to pick me up. They smiled at me, and their teeth were black and rotten.

They took me away to a place where we sat at an oval table, my mom on my left and my dad on my right. They smiled again and my mom's teeth were pearly white, but my dad's teeth were still black and rotten. This dream haunted me for the first fourteen years of my life. After each dream, strong emotions of fear and confusion would remain with me throughout the day.

When I was fourteen, my mom finally told me that they tried to abort me when abortions were illegal. I was delivered shortly after the botched abortion, but I was alive. My mom struggled to keep me alive because I was born at home and was extremely premature. My mom suffered all those years with the guilt of what she had allowed my dad and his sister talk her into, and she was so very sorry. I guess that's why, in my dream, her teeth became white again. My dad never showed any remorse, and I guess that's why what he felt came across as rotten teeth.

I forgave my mom immediately upon her revealing the abortion incident. I even tried to comfort her because I saw her anguish. Even at fourteen, I understood how she had suffered through the years because of this life-changing destructive decision to have an abortion.

I now understand the dream and the battle to hang on. Most importantly, I believe that even before birth we begin to store information in our subconscious, and we respond to what we have stored throughout life unless we re-program our brain. This re-programming must be designed to dump old destructive information and replace it with positive constructive information.

When I was a very young child, the abortion advo-

                              MARJORIE BARCOMB

cating aunt took me aside and told me I was a brat and then said that my parents never wanted me. I was crushed. When I asked my mom about what aunt Ida said, she cried and hugged me. Of course this was before I knew about the attempted abortion.

As a child, life at home was very stressful. My father continually told me that I was worthless and that I didn't earn my 'keeps.' As a consequence, I tried to eat as little as possible and remained a very skinny child. I was so skinny that the doctor who did our school exams sent a note home saying I suffered from malnutrition.

As children, my siblings and I worked extremely hard on a very unproductive dairy farm. My father did not appreciate our hard work. We were consistently and frequently told how stupid and how worthless we were. We were never praised for a job well done no matter how hard we tried. I guess this is why we all got good grades to prove to ourselves that we were not stupid and worthless. This doesn't work! What you have been told over and over remains in your subconscious even though it runs counter to reality.

We had to work especially hard during school summer vacations to gather and store the crops for the winter. I had to drive a big truck pulling a hay-loader when I was ten years old. I had to sit on the edge of the seat to reach the clutch. If I jerked the truck in the slightest or if I missed a spear of hay, my dad would literally come unglued and scream at me and threaten me for several minutes. With this, my heart would pound, my hands would shake, and I would have to try to control myself so that I wouldn't make any more mistakes.

One summer while taking in the crops, I had a severe case of the flu with all its side effects. My dad would not let me stay at home in bed. I had to work in the hayfield anyway. I'd have to jump off the load of hay frequently to take care of my sickness. Of course, I was screamed at every time I did. I started the summer weighing one hundred pounds and after working in the hayfield with the flu, I ended up weighing seventy-seven pounds. I just wanted to die. It was always good to get back to school because my school life was a bit better, but it was not the greatest either.

After my two eldest brothers left home, things turned for the worse. I was nine years old at the time. I guess my dad didn't dare to act out his most evil aggressions while they were still living at home. He became a tyrant! He'd beat my mom, knock her out, and leave her in a pool of blood. To torture her further he'd say, "I'm going to kill the kids." I lived in terror because I knew we were just nanoseconds from being killed. He'd wield a gun as he was making these threats. I used to run away and hide in a big concrete culvert. I'd stay in there for hours.

He always showed his disdain for females, and my sister and I were called very derogatory names because of it. We lived in constant terror. My fear of being murdered was intensified by the fact that I felt that I wasn't wanted anyway. Only my faith in God kept me going. School provided a safe haven, but I still carried my angst with me to school.

Fortunately or unfortunately, I attended kindergarten for three months, first grade for one day, and then on to second grade. I was still in an educational whirlwind when I passed second grade.

By the time I was in third grade I was two to three years younger than my classmates. To add to my already mixed-up life, most of my classmates ignored me, mistreated me, or laughed at me. They laughed at me because of my immaturity. They called me names because I was skinny; one name was spindle legs. They didn't want me on their academic or sports teams. I was never chosen by students who headed the spelling bees although I would have brought much to the team. They wouldn't play with me on the playground. I was alone and becoming more isolated, sad and bitter every day. Life was not fun.

High school brought with it a little reprieve from the earlier school days, but it was far from ideal. I learned to submerge myself in my school work and to look forward to the day when I could leave both school and home. I contemplated suicide, but I lacked the courage to go through with it.

As a result of my home life and my school life, I always felt that I wasn't wanted. After hearing my dad say that I was worthless over and over and threatening to kill me, I really developed a very low opinion of myself. I wanted to be accepted so badly that I worked hard in school where I excelled at everything I studied. Even when I received my doctorate degree with a 4.0 average, my dad said, "They have to give a certain number of degrees to women; they really don't earn them." All in all, I grew up to be a needy person; I just wanted to be accepted and loved. That can cause serious problems! Thank God, my mom taught me values that prevented me from doing something really stupid and/or destructive—but, my self esteem still suffered.

For many years I continued to fear and distrust my father. Finally, at age thirty-seven, I moved to the desert Southwest. On my way to work one morning, I was appreciating the view of the lettuce crops. I could see lettuce in various stages of growth. I thought of my life and the rocky stages that I had experienced. My mind raced back to the lettuce; I could see how care and nurturing produced great results. Just then, I looked back in my rear view mirror and saw the rising sun and the mountains and started to give thanks for the beauty of creation. At that moment, an awesome overpowering emotion rushed through me. It was like being re-born. At that moment, I decided that this was the beginning of my new life—that I would create my own continual nurturing, and not look back. I decided to break the rear view mirror of my life and keep only beautiful and constructive images in the forefront of my mind. I felt passionate about becoming who I wanted to be. I had given myself a big assignment, but I thought about the positive results I wanted for the rest of my life.

The first part of my assignment was to forgive my dad. This was very difficult even though I was almost three thousand miles from him. Miles don't separate emotions. It took three months of praying and soul searching to finally forgive him and get rid of that heavy albatross from around my neck. Once I had granted him total forgiveness, my life started to improve dramatically. I was ready for the next step.

The next thing I had to do was to concentrate on the nurturing and care that I learned from the lettuce crops. I decided to start my nurturing by saying nice things to

                                        MARJORIE BARCOMB

myself and about myself every day. I talked to myself; I talked to the mirror, and I talked out loud. To anyone else, I may have looked like I had a screw loose, but I didn't care; I was healing! I started to become my best friend and I liked the person I was becoming.

My life took a 180 degree turn. My self-esteem, my confidence, and self-worth started to get pulled from the pit. My negative and self-destructive thoughts were disappearing and they were being replaced with positive constructive thoughts as if by osmosis. I began to look forward to each new day, and I started focusing on new goals and objectives I wanted to fulfill in my life.

I was already writing objectives in my detailed lesson plans for my chemistry class every day. I was a dedicated teacher and wanted to help my chemistry students clearly understand the underlying principles of chemistry. Plainly, if I could insure success for my students, applying the same process would insure success for me in achieving my own personal goals and objectives.

My next step was to write lesson plans for my life. They served as my road-map or trip plan for my successful and happy future. It was almost miraculous to see and feel the progress I made as a result of these *written* plans. Evaluating my progress served as a motivating factor to keep me moving forward, and it showed me whether I had to modify or adjust my objectives.

As I look back at the steps I took to propel me into my new life, I'm reminded that just as most scientific principles are simple and practical, *The Formula,* too, is simple and practical.

After using the steps in the formula to overcome obstacles and struggles in my life, I realized that *The Formula* was something I should share with everyone. *The Formula* can change lives. Now, my hope is to help others move into a happier and more constructive future as quickly and as effortlessly as possible.

ON THE SURFACE, WHO DO YOU THINK YOU ARE?

"Some people, no matter how old they get, never lose their beauty—they merely move it from their faces to their hearts."[1]

"There is only one way to achieve happiness on this terrestrial ball and that is to have either a clear conscience or none at all."[2]

Have you ever thought about why some people are so successful while others are not? How do you feel about your degree of success? What is it that makes each individual unique?

We are each unique individuals as a result of the combination of our genetics and our upbringing. Some of what we are, we have no control over because these characteristics are genetically programmed in our DNA. For example, we have no control over our eye color, hair color, stature, and many other physical attributes. But there is so very much that we do have control over, and that is very exciting. It is an unfortunate fact that many people feel they do not have control over their lives; they feel at a loss to make changes because of learned helplessness. There is a solution to this dilemma, and it starts with you. This chapter will give you the tools for self-examination into your past which will give you insight as to why you have become the person that you are today. Once you have determined what got you to this point, you will have a platform from which to start making changes in your life.

You see, your brain is like a giant computer. Since birth, everything you have perceived with your senses, whether it was what you have heard, felt, tasted, seen, or smelled has been stored in your brain. Even though you may not remember, all this incoming sensory data that you've stored remains there like a sleeping giant. The consequence of these stored messages is that you react to them and don't always know why. The messages that you've received through the years from your parents, teachers, friends, siblings, and others have played a major role in determining who you have become and are the reason that you think of yourself as you do.

When I was nine months old, I remember my mom showing me a stuffed animal. It was a gray elephant. It was before Christmas, and she just couldn't wait to show it to me. I remember crying and hearing her say, in my first language, that she couldn't give it to me because it was a Christmas present and that she had to hide it before my older siblings came home from school. I remember thinking that I just wanted to hold it.

On another occasion when I was about a year and a half, I learned how to climb out of my crib. Now this was a traumatic time for me because it was the first time my mom slapped my behind, and it really hurt, especially where her hand hit below the diaper. I can remember how it burned. I couldn't understand why she said that I would get hurt if I fell out of the crib, but she was hurting me. I wanted to talk, but I couldn't. I remember thinking, "I wish I could

                                    MARJORIE BARCOMB

talk because I would tell her that I know how to get out of the crib and even if I fell it wouldn't hurt as much as the spanking." Clearly, I could think in terms of language, but I couldn't talk. These images are etched in my brain. Undoubtedly there are many other images etched in my brain that I do not remember.

Most of what happened when I was a very young child I do not remember, but I do remember these two occasions very clearly. This makes me understand without question that all our experiences are stored in our brain, and we sometimes respond to them and don't even know why.

You may be familiar with the old computer saying, "Garbage in, garbage out." This is also true of our brain computer. You also may have heard sayings such as, "Like father, like son," or "The apple doesn't fall far from the tree." Parents tend to tell their children what they heard when they were children; consequently, the children grow up receiving the same messages as their parents did when they grew up. The result is they behave or respond in a similar fashion to their parents or caregivers in good times and bad. If there are things you don't like about the cycle you have been handed, breaking the chain is up to you. You can do it!

The computer was designed after the human-brain; therefore, we can draw inferences from their similarities. The brain is a very special giant computer because it has an added attribute—it stores emotions connected to incoming sense data; consequently, we need to take a close analytical look at this incoming data and determine what it is doing to our emotional health, to our physical health, and to our degree of success—in essence, to our lives.

When consistent messages come into our brain over time, great neural pathways or super-highways are formed. When these messages are consistent and positive, they yield good or great results depending on the frequency and intensity of this incoming data. This generally results in happy and successful individuals with great self-esteem, confidence, and leadership abilities.

When the messages are mostly positive but contain some glitches, such as inconsistencies in the incoming data, the neural pathways that result are not as efficient; they seem to have some little side roads, and the result may be basically positive but also may tend to yield some inconsistent behaviors. These individuals are baffled about what to do. Their focus is a bit foggy. They get side-tracked easily. Their behaviors are not always consistent and clear. They find it easier to follow someone who has a clear sense of purpose. A little re-programming can quickly help these individuals to become more successful. "Whatever the mind of man can conceive, it can achieve."[3]

When the incoming sense data is mostly negative and destructive, we see results that exhibit low self-esteem, low self-worth, lack of confidence, and destructive behaviors. These individuals need a tremendous amount of reprogramming. But, the good news is that much is possible if an individual truly wants to change his or her life.

Remember, we can't help what we have had programmed as a result of the incoming messages from our caregivers, but we can change how we let it affect our lives now. Many of us have suffered through traumatic beginnings or events but have, through effort and education, learned to rise above our circumstances. Others need help in getting positive re-programming.

Some programming may have occurred even before birth. If so, we started storing information in our subconscious even before we were born. Dr. Manny Alvarez, a Fox News contributor, reported on a Netherland's study which was conducted on one hundred women and their unborn children. The results of the study showed that unborn babies of about thirty weeks gestation developed a short term memory of about ten minutes, but at thirty-four weeks gestation they had short term memory up to four weeks.[4,5] I'm happy to hear of this research because my own personal experience indicated my unborn memory being demonstrated in dreams that lasted over a period of fourteen years.

Getting back to messages, many of the messages we have stored are good, or we have good programming, but many of the messages we have received through the years are negative, hurtful, and self defeating. Just listen to what a parent says to a child. Count the number of negative comments made versus the number of positive comments. Chances are you'll find that close to ninety percent of the comments are negative. A child hears the word no thousands and thousands of times before reaching adulthood.

Are you ready to learn how to change, modify, amend, or dump old programming that has resulted from self-defeating, inappropriate, and/or destructive messages you have received in the past?

While dumping old programs we need to fill the void with good programming. It's like getting rid of a computer virus and then re-programming your computer to make it more efficient and reliable. I think we have all dealt with computer problems and know how refreshing it is to get rid of the bad and replace it with the good clean programs. The exciting thing is that the computer with good programming is always valid and consistent; we know exactly what to expect when we open particular programs. It is like a person with intense focus. When your brain computer is correctly programmed, you too, become a person who demonstrates a consistent, dependable, clear sense of direction.

Are you ready to find out what you have stored in your brain computer? If so, find a nice comfortable quiet nook where you will not be disturbed. You will need a pad of paper and a pen or pencil. Now, it is time for you to thoughtfully ponder the following questions:

1. In your mind, which parts of your character need improvement?
2. What do you enjoy doing?
3. What is your real passion–that which you truly desire to achieve?
4. What do you consider success?
5. Which parts of your character make you proud?
6. If money or time was no object, what would you be doing?

Now, sit back, close your eyes, and think about your answers to these questions making sure that you can remember your thoughts. Take your time because what you are about to discover is very important. Do not discount your first thoughts because you thought them first for a reason. Now go back and re-read each question, but this time write down your answers.

Next, look at your questions again, but this time say your answers out loud, and listen to what you say. Now compare your initial thoughts to your written answers and then to your spoken answers.

Finally, re-read and answer the questions out loud while looking in the mirror. Compare your new answers to your previous answers. Notice how your answers have changed from your silent answers. You may even start laughing at yourself as you see how your answers change going from silent to written to out loud to out loud looking in the mirror.

Are you now asking yourself, "Why are my thoughts so negative? My silent answers make no rational sense." You are correct! Many times our silent answers make no sense at all and are not based on fact. Your responses come from your subconscious programming. Your subconscious is at work here, and your subconscious is developed from all your life experiences, even those you don't remember.

Think of the thoughts that you have thought so many times, over and over, almost like a broken record. Are you thinking," I could never accomplish…" or "I'll never be successful enough to…" or "I'm just not smart enough…" or "I hate myself because I never do anything right"? If you keep saying these things over and over in your mind, they become a self-fulfilling prophecy. We attract our thoughts. If we are negative, we attract negative people and negative circumstances. If we are positive, we attract positive people and positive circumstances. Which do you choose?

Now that you have completed this activity, did you notice that when saying the answers out loud as compared to saying them silently, you didn't beat up on yourself so badly? Are you asking yourself, "Why did I beat up on myself when left alone with my thoughts?" or "Why are my thoughts so negative?" "I'm too embarrassed to speak so negatively out loud because the facts don't fit." Most people's silent thoughts do beat up on themselves, and it is quite normal to do so. It is highly probable that when over ninety percent of what you heard growing up was negative, your overall programming is negative. Most of us have heard, "No" thousands and thousands of times while growing up. Your brain computer's memory bank may contain a lot more negative messages than positive messages. Many of the negative messages may have been suppressed to the point that you no longer remember them, but they are still there! Using a technique to erase or 'dump' destructive messages and replace them with positive constructive thoughts will not only improve your self-concept but also your ability to pursue your highest aspirations.

Did you notice that in the chapters dealing with universal standards that we should all live by, in the practice section at the end of each standard, you were asked to make 3X5 cards with positive statements written on them? The purpose for this was to re-program your brain to incorporate principles that people of great character demonstrate. The neat part about doing this exercise is that you don't have to consciously erase the old bad programming. The

                               MARJORIE BARCOMB

consistent input of positive messages eventually will erase or at least overpower the old negative stuff. I casually call this 'pump and dump;' that is, you pump in the positive and that in essence starts to dump out the negative. Your subconscious will begin to react to the new re-programming. The crucial element here is that you continually repeat, over and over, the new messages that you want as part of your new programming. Again, you cannot miss a day. The Rule of Thirty Days says that if you miss a day, you must start over again until you have repeated the positive affirmation for thirty consecutive days. Make many of the positive affirmations part of your permanent daily regimen. Say nice things to yourself and about yourself every day. Your goal is to build new permanent neural pathways that carry consistent, positive information.

We are all born on fire to live our dreams and aspirations, but most of us slowly got beaten down to think and live in the box. I marvel at the freshness of thoughts and dreams of first graders, but unfortunately the flame has been partially or totally extinguished by the time they are in fourth grade. What happened? Too many "No's" and not enough encouragement has finally beaten their thinking into the box their parents and teachers think is in their best interest. Children whose parents work in the fields aspire to be the boss in the field. Their initial dreams of becoming president are slowly eroded away by their circumstances and what they hear. Their programming is now set in concrete, their self-esteem is in the abyss, and their confidence is all but gone. Their motivation died a long time ago, and the thrill of joining a gang looks better and better as each day passes. Great news—we can re-ignite the flame, we can make a difference, we can chip away at that concrete, and we can revive our dreams and aspirations!

If you are not where you would like to be with respect to your success and happiness, it may be because your life experiences have affected you in a way that has stifled your motivation to achieve in those areas. You can overcome!

HOW HAVE YOUR LIFE EXPERIENCES AFFECTED YOU?

"I cannot imagine how anyone can say, "I'm weak" and then remain so. After all, if you know it, why not fight against it? Why not try to train your character?"

Do you yearn for success and happiness? Do you feel emptiness in your life? Are you just plain unhappy with the direction your life-path seems to have taken you? If so, you are not alone. If time and money was no object, most people would not be doing what they are doing now. If you can honestly say that if you had time and money, you would be doing exactly what you are doing, then you may be living your dreams. If you would like to make changes in your life, you are the only one who can do it. You cannot expect to keep doing what you are now doing and get a different result.

You may have heard the expressions, "When I get rich" or "When I win the lottery," or "When my ship comes in," or "When I get ahead." You'll notice that individuals who make such comments continue to do what they have always done in the past and expect a different result. A little secret here: *it doesn't happen!* If you expect to see a change in your life, you must change what you are doing; and the only way you can change what you are doing is to change how you think.

What's holding you back? Do you suffer from fear of rejection or fear of failure? Do you think you are just not smart enough, talented enough, or that your looks will prevent you from succeeding? Do you feel helpless and don't know where to turn? Do you think there is no hope? Do you feel trapped in your circumstances? Remember, if you have serious depression or other serious emotional distress, see a doctor! But, if you feel that you just don't fit the mold that your parents and teachers expected you to fit, what follows may be of interest.

As a teacher who was determined that my students would truly understand the principles of chemistry, I tried every possible technique, including both those I had studied and those I thought in my heart would work. The heart wins out! While teaching chemistry, I made sure to cover each underlying principle of chemistry at least five times using a different approach each time. This required a lot of research and a lot of lesson planning on my part! We all have different learning styles and/or combinations of learning styles that make us unique individuals. The gift for me was that I began to see 'why' my students were becoming so successful.

Parents, teachers, and others tend to impart knowledge the way they were taught. Unfortunately, most teachers are linear thinkers; this is why they enjoy teaching. The peculiar thing is that most students are random thinkers. It is no wonder, that in many cases, both have such a hard time.

I used to do a little experiment with my graduate students who were teachers. I'd ask them to close their eyes and visualize three apples, then take out a sheet of paper

                    MARJORIE BARCOMB

and draw the three apples as they had visualized them. Then I carried my little experiment to an alternative school setting during my summer break from the university.

I decided I would donate one month of my time trying to help high school students that could not make it in the normal high school. They were placed in an alternative school and deemed too tough to handle. I was told that most of them had discipline or socialization problems.

The first day, I started conversing with these young adults as though they were normal human beings–because they were, and I told them I wanted to do a little experiment. I told them that I do this same experiment with my graduate students and that I bet they could do better.

I asked them to visualize three apples and then to draw them on a sheet of paper. I was absolutely astonished because every student had a totally different picture. One had three apples on an apple tree, another three apples in a bowl, another three randomly drawn apples, (1 with a worm, 1 half eaten with perfect teeth marks, and the last one whole). I could go on and on about the uniqueness of each student's work. They were indeed random thinkers and didn't draw their three apples exactly the same size, in a neat little row, with all the stems pointing in the same direction as the teachers working on their masters' degrees did.

No wonder we don't know who we are or where we are headed. We have these people trying to teach us in black and white, top to bottom, left to right on a sheet of two-dimensional paper. They just don't seem to get it! They have to learn how to pull that information off the paper and back into our beautiful three-dimensional world–apples on a tree, apples in a bowl, and apples partially eaten. Instead, many teachers and parents alike take our beautiful three-dimensional world and make it that dull! Oh, and it's the children's fault. And, you wonder why you haven't achieved your dreams. You may just be a square peg trying to fit in a round hole. Whatever you do, don't blame your parents and/or your teachers; they were just trying to help you the best way they knew how. They simply repeated what was taught to them.

So what kind of a peg are you? How have positive experiences and positive reinforcement molded your life? The best way to attack this question is to lie down in a quiet private place and start to re-live your life. Try to remember back when you were one year old, then two, and so on. You may not remember anything before you went to school and that's normal, but go back as far as you can. When you get to the point of your first memories, try to re-establish your surroundings, your furniture, your house, your church, your car, your family, your friends, your relatives, your appearance, your pets, the foods you ate, the things you did, and the clothes you wore. The most important part is the memory of the human interaction you had. Do you remember any specific instances that were positive, fun, and motivational? Do you remember any specific instances that were negative, demeaning, and/or distressing?

Do this for each year of your life. Take a notebook, and on opposite facing pages write on one page all the positive experiences, positive communications, and positive reinforcement you remember for each year. On the opposite

     MARJORIE BARCOMB

facing page, write all the negative experiences, negative communications, and negative reinforcement you remember for that year. Chances are in your early years most of these memories will involve your parents and your siblings. Try to remember how everyone around you talked to you and how you felt as a child. Also, try to remember body language such as, the look and how that made you feel. It took me three months to do this; therefore, I suggest that you finish reading the book then come back to this section and complete this activity.

After you have written all your memories, go back and examine each one, then ask yourself the following questions:

- In each instance where you received praise or any other positive attention, what was the reason? How did you feel? How many times do these feelings re-visit you? Which ones do you still feel today?
- In each instance where you were corrected or belittled, what were the extenuating circumstances? How did you feel? How many times do these feelings re-visit you? Which of these feelings still 'haunt' you? Which of these feelings do you find yourself repeating over and over in your mind?

In the last chapter you probably discovered that your first thoughts about yourself were considerably more negative than your out-loud discourse about yourself. Now, can you tie some of these negative feelings to instances you wrote about in your notebook? If you can, it is time for you to start forgiving anyone who has hurt you and/or damaged your self-confidence and your self-esteem. By forgiving them, you have an opportunity to let go of both the instances that you remembered and wrote in your notebook, and even the instances that you do not remember that are buried in your subconscious. It's the first step in learning to let go.

How has your negative programming affected you? What thoughts go through your mind as you ponder your belief or lack of belief in yourself? Now all this can change for you. I'm not saying that you will become the happiest most successful person in the world, but by improving your life significantly, you can make great strides in the pursuit of your dreams and aspirations.

PART 3

WHO DO YOU WANT TO BE?

BUILDING NEW NEURAL PATHWAYS: REPLACING NEGATIVE OR DESTRUCTIVE THOUGHTS AND HABITS WITH POSITIVE CONSTRUCTIVE ONES

"Be very careful about what you think. Your thoughts run your life."[1]

To establish new neural pathways that will wipe out your destructive thoughts and habits, you must understand that you are worthy, you are valuable, and you deserve to make your life the best that it can be—successful and happy. Unleash the Army of helpers in your brain. Let them help you fight for your future.

You may have already noticed that in your previous practice sessions you were asked you to do three things. First, you were asked to do self-talk or positive affirmations. Second, you were asked to visualize a situation or scenario wherein you were part of an unfolding drama. You were asked to mentally envision yourself as being the person you want to become, picturing yourself with all the emotions and feelings that emerged from the mental imagery. Third, you were asked to carefully monitor your actions on a daily basis and to evaluate what you had done each day. What exactly is it that makes these three criteria so powerful?

CRITERION #1: POSITIVE SELF-TALK OR POSITIVE AFFIRMATIONS

Everyone who has become extremely successful has either accidentally or intentionally made use of positive self-talk or positive affirmations. One of my favorite self-talk affirmations was when Mohammed Ali used to say, "I am the king." He didn't start out as the king. In looking at his youth, you can quickly observe that he had to work hard to get the degree of success that he attained. He took his self-talk so seriously that he shared it with the world. Look at the results he got. You may say that he was lucky or one in a million, but that is just not the case. Countless people have used self-talk or positive affirmations to improve their lives. Self-talk is a critical element in helping ordinary people achieve extraordinary success.

There are many individuals who will say they tried the self-help technique of positive affirmations or positive self-talk, and it doesn't work. Why is this so? They have missed some of the essential elements of effective self-talk. The effectiveness of your self-talk depends on the quality of self-talk that you practice. The factors that will determine your degree of success include the following:

- staying determined and passionate about your improvement
- writing and re-writing your positive self-talk statements
- keeping your self-talk or affirmations positive and in the present tense
- making your self-talk believable to your subconscious mind

- practicing frequently and with focus
- arousing your feelings and emotions connected to your self-talk

You must eagerly want to see change in your life, and you must be willing to do whatever it takes, as long as it takes. If you don't have the passion to make this commitment, the degree of your results will wane. I know you are worth it. If you need help in this area, you may have to start your self-talk with sayings that will convince your sub-conscious of your value. Remember the saying, "God doesn't make any junk." That means you! Get passionate about what you want to achieve in your life and give it all you got. Unchain yourself from your past and reach for the freedom to turn your dreams into reality. You deserve it!

Never put off until tomorrow what you can do today. This is also true for your positive self-talk. It must be in the present tense in order to work for you. If you say, "I will exercise" that's a far cry from, "I exercise" or "I choose to exercise." The first statement gives you license to wait because you are talking about the future. Keep your self-talk in a positive vein. Rather than saying, "I'm not over-weight" say "I choose to be slender." It is incredible the difference in what you feel when making a statement more positive. You do not want your subconscious to hear the word, overweight. You want your subconscious to hear the word, slender. Notice the difference? We attract what we say.

Practicing your self-talk statements frequently throughout the day will make them more effective. Planning your self-talk sessions will keep you focused and on track. Writing your positive self-talk on 3 X 5 cards or post it notes and sticking them to the bathroom mirror works well and gives you a jump start for the rest of the day. Additionally, you may write your self-talk statements in a small notebook, and read them throughout the day. The notebook idea is great because your positive affirmations are at your fingertips when you need them most as you encounter issues of the day.

Self-talk is done to pass information from your conscious mind to your subconscious so that it becomes part of your reality. That is why most self-talk statements begin with the word, I. Your self-talk must be personal. As children, we have all heard some things over and over until we believed they were true even though we could rationalize that they were not true. For example, let's assume you were told that you were stupid and worthless over and over until you believed it. Then upon going to school, you were always on the honor roll. You knew that you were not stupid, but you still may have had the emotions and feelings that you were. Conversely, your subconscious mind may have a terrible time accepting something that it knows is not true or is totally unrealistic. In these cases, we have to make our self-talk reasonable and couch it in such a way that our subconscious mind can accept it. An example would be if you decided you wanted to be an NFL football player but you were a fifty-year-old female. Unrealistic! Your subconscious will laugh at you. In another situation, let's assume you would like to quit drinking alcohol. If you say, "I don't drink," you may not get much mileage with your subcon-

                        MARJORIE BARCOMB

scious; but if you say, "I choose not to drink," your subconscious can accept it.

Pay attention to areas where you can acquire continuous improvement such as your self-esteem, your self-worth, or your confidence. You don't want your self-talk to be a dead end. Saying, "I have great self-worth" implies you have arrived. If you say, "My self-worth improves each day," you leave room for growth.

There is some disagreement on the duration and intensity of effective self-talk. I choose to stick with Shad Helmstetter's Rule of Thirty Days that I have mentioned in several chapters. Personally, I want to be sure that my subconscious has accepted my self-talk as truth so that my subconscious will provide very consistent, automatic responses. There is nothing magical about the Rule of Thirty Days. Keep using your self-talk long after you have encountered some success. You want your self-talk to become part of the fabric of your life for your entire future.

I also agree with Helmstetter that each important word in the saying needs to be stressed. In addition, I feel that it is imperative for you to attach the appropriate emotion with your self-talk expression. Just saying the affirmations like a robot without emotion will not be effective. Your subconscious doesn't lead you to react on what you have told it, but on the emotion connected to the message.

At this point, you may be asking yourself, "How many positive self-talk statements should I be practicing each day?" The answer is, "It is up to you." Some people prefer to deal with only a few of their top priority self-talk statements at a time. After finding success they add more statements to their list. Others love multi-tasking and practice many self-talk statements each day. We are all different. Think about it, and then do what you think will bring you the most success.

CRITERION #2: MENTAL IMAGERY OR VISUALIZING

Have you ever been accused of day-dreaming? Do you remember when your mind used to wander, and you believed in your passions only to have a teacher or someone in authority tell you to *get your feet back on the ground* or *get your head out of the clouds*. With this kind of feedback, your inquisitive nature about all that God has created and given us may have eroded little by little over time until you became just like everyone else. It's time to take back what is rightfully yours–your vivid, exciting, almost magical dreams! After completing your positive self-talk or positive affirmations, it's time to start picturing yourself as the person you want to become. This helps you to connect the appropriate emotion to your affirmation statements.

Visualizing or day-dreaming provides the subconscious with clear, emotional, committed, competent, etc. pictures of yourself being the person you aspire to become. When the universal standards that you read about earlier become part of the fabric of your subconscious, you will find yourself well-grounded as a person of principle, a person of character. It is only with this foundation that you can become fully free to choose, to seek, and to attain the rest of your dreams and to do so without fear of consequences. You are indeed ready to face the world.

Vivid mental images motivate you on your quest to reach the pinnacle of your dreams. As you build your character and your confidence, you will attract people who will become not only your friends, but your 'reference group' or 'circle of empowerment.' The emotions and feelings resulting from your mental images will determine how you behave, and your behavior will determine your success and happiness. You begin to see yourself in a different light!

Since many sports require both a strong mental game as well as physical skills, numerous coaches preach that sports are close to ninety percent mental and ten percent physical. When only fractions of a second separate first place from second place, it is important that the coaches use every tool at their disposal. They have resorted to mental imagery because it works. It may give the athlete the edge to beat out the competition. Areas where athletes use mental imagery include practicing specific skills, improving confidence, and increasing endurance.

Collectively your mind and emotions provide the ammunition for action. Just as any ammunition, it can be used for good or for evil. Guard your thoughts and always keep them positive and in sync with the universal standards of civility.

In Rhonda Byrne's book, *The Secret*, she says that if you visualize and think happy thoughts, the "Law of Attraction" will attract what you want in your life.[2] Lazy people love to hear this. What Byrne says is partly true, but simply thinking happy thoughts is not enough to change your thoughts into deeds and your deeds into a new lifestyle. It isn't that simple; certainly you attract people and ideas and things that you think about, but life is a little thing that gets in the way. We cannot control all our daily circumstances, but we can control our thoughts, our morals, our words, our motivation, our anger, our desires, our dedication, our work ethic, our goals and objectives, and our focus and persistence. When you are a highly principled person, you will attract people of good moral fiber. When you think positive thoughts, you attract people who think positive thoughts, but that is just one ingredient in getting you on the road to fulfill your goals and objectives which will ultimately lead you to a successful and happy life.

Another key ingredient is continual self-development. Thinking without action gets you nowhere. Simply thinking about and talking about a destination does not automatically get you there by telekinesis. It takes courage, fortitude and action in the direction of your goals. It takes courage to press on when life seems to be running into more obstacles than you think you can handle.

This requires work on your part. But you will attract people and ideas by your thoughts because your thoughts rule your behavior, and your behavior attracts, is neutral, or repels people and constructive ideas.

You will find that as you practice using positive self-talk and positive mental imagery, you will be gifted with intuitive insights that seem to come at you like lightning bolts. Your brain will make the connections to disclose ideas and solutions for you that you never dreamed you could come up with before. Your brain is such a miraculous organ, and it responds uniquely to stimuli. As you input your self-talk statements and mental images, your brain sorts it all out

                    MARJORIE BARCOMB

and comes up with elegant synthesized answers that are simply amazing!

CRITERION #3: MONITOR AND EVALUATE YOUR ACTIONS ON A DAILY BASIS

Each morning say your chosen self-talk, create or re-enact your mental imagery, and then armed with positive energy, face the day. You will find that there are many areas in which you would like to set goals and objectives. As a consequence, your self-talk may seem a bit overwhelming. Prioritize your goals and then look at the objectives you must complete to get you on track to realize the achievement of those goals. You will be learning a clear, easy to understand strategy to deal with your goals and objectives in later chapters. Once you understand how this is done, select the goals you want to work on, write your positive self-talk statements, and create your mental images that will help you to be victorious at fulfilling your goals. You will work on these goals concurrently with the universal standards of civility.

As I said earlier, setting and achieving goals is futile if you are not well-grounded in the universal standards of civility. As a consequence, pick one standard that you want to work on first. Work on that standard for one full month; don't miss a day. Re-read the chapter that deals with that standard, and concentrate on its value at home, at work, at school, out shopping, at church, while traveling, while enjoying recreation, and everywhere you go and in everything you do. Keep that standard or value in the forefront of your mind when you are with your siblings, your children, your parents, your co-workers, your spouse, your teammates, your pastor, your acquaintances, and strangers. Live your life immersed in that standard for thirty full days.

Each month select another standard until after seven months you have worked your way through all the standards. You may want to break the chapter on respect into two parts, with one month on respect for self and another month on respect for others and the environment. If you choose to break this into two parts, you will still complete re-programming your brain in the universal standards of civility in eight months. It took you a lot longer than eight months to get the belief system you now possess, so eight months is a small price to pay to become a highly principled person.

Let's assume that you are already a highly principled person. Just doing the self-talk, creating the mental imagery, and monitoring and evaluating your actions for each standard for a full month will help you tremendously in being a role model for others. Now that's truly worth the effort. It's beneficial to over-learn doing what is right and doing it for the right reasons.

If you are a parent, this is a great opportunity to teach your children the universal standards of civility and to show them the benefit of possessing good character. This can be a lot of fun; make a game out of preparing your self-talk cards and sharing your mental pictures. Children have vivid imaginations; they may be teaching you. Together, you may choose to make bumper stickers of phrases that stick in your mind on strips of white paper using colored markers. Put your bumper stickers on the refrigerator so your children can see them every day. Make sure they learn to feel good about being good and doing what is right. Conversely, they should learn that it does not feel good when doing things that run counter to good behavior.

After you have determined your positive self-talk statements and have created your mental images, be deliberate about your actions. Each day monitor your actions with respect to your self-talk. In the evening evaluate what you said and did as a consequence of your self-talk. Now is not the time to give up. Are you a wimp? Or are you a person of steel? Are you like a mighty hurricane? When you stick to a certain number of high priority goals for one full month, you will be astonished how much you can achieve because of your actions. Ask your coworkers, your spouse, or any other person close to you if they see a difference in your behavior and/or attitude.

PERSEVERANCE IN THE FACE OF CHALLENGE FACILITATES YOUR SUCCESS

"When you get into a tight place and everything goes against you, till it seems as though you could not hang on a minute longer, never give up then, for that is just the place and time that the tide will turn."[1]

"Nothing can take the place of persistence. Talent will not; nothing is more common than unsuccessful men with talent. Genius will not; unrewarded genius is almost a proverb. Education will not; the world is full of educated derelicts. Persistence and determination alone are omnipotent."[2]

Even though you may be working diligently on your positive self-talk, your mental imagery, and monitoring and evaluating your actions, you will continue to face challenges. That's life. Don't be a baby. Persevere no matter what!

If you feel overwhelmed at any point keep in mind Rome wasn't built in a day. Every day that you see even the smallest improvement means you are going in the right direction. Becoming the success that you desire is not based on luck or talent; it is based on an intense passion to succeed and hard work.

When you see successful people who have made it, you tend to think that they were lucky or talented. They probably just stuck to their dreams longer than you have. Most successful people didn't get to where they are overnight. We often think that they are smarter than we are, and we go back to our old self-defeating negative self-talk. You have just as much ability as anyone else; you just have to persevere. At one time, I taught teachers how to teach gifted and talented students. One thing that still sticks in my mind is that everyone is more talented or gifted than ninety-three percent of the population in some area of their life. This means that you can do something better than ninety-three percent of the population. Your job is to find out what it is. Talent and luck help a lot, but perseverance will take you to your destination. What you do each day should not be an end in itself but part of a life-long journey to success and happiness. Enjoy the journey! "Think of a postage stamp; it sticks to one thing till it gets there."[3]

Thomas Edison, in his quest to make a lead storage battery, found over one thousand ways that didn't work. Did he give up? What did he say? He said, "I've found one thousand ways that do not work." He did not say, "I was unsuccessful." He continued working until he was successful with the storage battery, as well as the electric light bulb, which took over five hundred attempts. In Thomas Edison's words, "Many of life's failures are people who did not realize how close they were to success when they gave up."[4]

Success isn't always easy, that's why I tell you to search your heart for the dreams that have been squelched, and become passionate about what you want to achieve and the direction you want your life to take.

When things go wrong as they sometimes will;

                    MARJORIE BARCOMB

When the road you're trudging seems all uphill;
When the funds are low, and the debts are high
And you want to smile, but have to sigh;
When care is pressing you down a bit-
Rest if you must, but do not quit.
Success is failure turned inside out;
The silver tint of the clouds of doubt;
And you can never tell how close you are
It may be near when it seems so far;
So stick to the fight when you're hardest hit-
It's when things go wrong that you must not quit.[5]

Use your self-talk to prepare yourself for adversity and challenges. Say things like, "I never give up." "I love a challenge." "I don't get discouraged; I always find a plan B." If you can't climb the mountain, go around it, tunnel through it, or fly over it, but get to the other side if that is your destination. Say, "There are multiple solutions to every problem; I just have to find one that works–just one."

Now picture yourself as a mighty hurricane–you are unstoppable. No matter what gets in your path, you manage to continue on to your predetermined goal. Feel the strength you have to overcome any and all road blocks. It's exhilarating; it's invigorating; and it's exciting. You are in control of your life. There is no going back to the poor me syndrome.

You will find that as you program your brain to be unstoppable, it gets easier and easier. You do not waste your time and energy thinking about the obstacles; you learn to use your time and energy wisely—to focus on possible solutions. You grow from adversity and from your mistakes.

Mistakes are not failures unless you let them be. Mistakes should be looked at as lessons in life—learning from hard knocks.

"Your greatest personal asset can be your willingness to persevere longer than anyone else. In fact, your persistence is a true measure of your belief in yourself and your ability to succeed."[6]

Your self-discipline is a quality that will have a major impact on your willingness to persevere. "If you will be hard on yourself, life will be easy on you. But if you insist upon being easy on yourself, life is going to be very hard on you."[7] Another fitting quote in describing self-discipline is "the ability to make yourself do what you should do, when you should do it, whether you like it or not."[8]

Each evening as you evaluate what you have done during the day, ask yourself whether you exhibited perseverance and determination when confronted with obstacles. Did you look for alternate solutions? Make sure to praise yourself even for the smallest improvement. "Many strokes, though with a little axe can tear down the hardest oak."[9] Your improvement is like a freight train; it takes off slowly, but when it gets a head of steam, watch-out. The momentum you build will keep you going even if you have a bad week or face other obstacles further on down the road.

PART 4

HOW DO YOU GET FROM WHO YOU
ARE TO WHO YOU WANT TO BE?

THE VALUE OF WRITING YOUR DREAM STATEMENT AND OF SETTING GOALS AND OBJECTIVES

*"Whatever you take in your
hand to do, remember the goal
and you shall never stray."*[1]

"It is necessary to try to always do better than yourself; this task should last as long as life."[2]

In Part 2, you gained insight into where your life has taken you and whether or not you feel you are headed in the right direction. You may not know exactly how to confront and triumph over your past, to make the necessary changes to become the person you would like to be. I am convinced that I have found the formula for success. I wrote this chapter to explain the formula for success that should help immensely in your quest to fulfilling your successful and happy future—and to do so with simplicity and ease. The first step in the formula for success includes creating your dream statement, an overarching umbrella statement which will assist you in developing reasonable short-term objectives and long-term goals. These three factors (your dream statement, your short-term objectives, and your long-term goals) are necessary to head you in the right direction. These three things dictate marching orders to the millions of neurons in your brain to assist you as you embark on a new chapter in your life. Incredibly this seems to happen without much thought or effort on your part. It is absolutely amazing how powerful your brain is if you are willing to give it a chance. You have awesome abilities that you probably have never given a chance to flourish.

You may gain a greater appreciation and determination for what you are about to set in motion by looking at two scenarios:

1. Would you enjoy going to court represented by an attorney that is not adequately prepared, one who has not prepared the necessary questions nor developed the case properly? Would that be a scary scenario? How would you feel about a situation like that? Would you have respect for that attorney or the law profession? Do you feel that this attorney has incorporated the timeless standards that you read about earlier?

2. Would you like to go to the operating room where the surgeon does not have all the materials available that are required to perform the operation correctly? Assume that the doctor has not gone over the strategy he or she plans to use in performing the surgical procedure. What can you say about this physician's level of moral development?

We would demand more from the individuals in the aforementioned scenarios. Therefore, if you want to be successful, you must be determined to do what is necessary to get you there, and to do so with seriousness of purpose. What is so exciting about the plan you are about to read is that it is fun, motivational, worthwhile, and easy to execute.

Your dream statement will be your master plan for success. From your dream statement or master plan, your goals and objectives will follow as a logical consequence because doing what you desire to do or are passionate about just comes naturally.

You will learn to develop and use a simple and organized blueprint for successful attainment of your short-term objectives and long-term goals. You will also look at potential road-blocks or obstacles and develop a proactive plan to mitigate these potential impediments so that you may realize your dreams. You will then look at what materials and/or resources you need to fulfill your objective, and finally you will work through a feedback loop which will help you to assess your degree of success and determine what to do next.

Part 4 Includes the Following:

- Writing your Dream Statement–your Master Plan
- Writing your short-term objectives, developing a strategy for success, facing road-blocks, listing required materials/resources, setting a time-line, and developing an assessment loop.
- Writing your long-term goals, developing a strategy for success, facing road-blocks, listing required materials/resources, setting a time-line, and developing an assessment loop.

WRITING YOUR DREAM STATEMENT

Your dream statement is really a master plan or a mission statement, but I call it a dream statement because too many people get stuck in the box when they write their personal master plan or a mission statement. I call it your dream statement because it is meant to let you think out of the box so that you may realize your dreams and aspirations. True success comes from living your life doing the things you are passionate about. Work should not be work!! That is not to say that your work should not be productive—on the contrary. But for you, your productive work should be fun and motivational. You should be excited when you get up in the morning to face a new day doing the things you love to do.

Your dream statement should state who you want to be and what you want your purpose in life to be, and it should do so in a nutshell. It should not go on and on. It should be direct and clearly stated. You may exclaim, "I don't know where to start!" I will give you some examples of dream statements from which you may select sections that are appropriate for you.

If we were to brainstorm some characteristics or attributes that you would like to enhance and/or develop as you pursue your personal quest for success and happiness, our list might look like the list below. You may also want to review the timeless standards of civility as you prepare your own personal list.

I've developed two dream statements that will give you an idea as to what a dream statement might look like. Feel free to use all or any part of these samples as you write your personal dream statement to fit your perception of what you want to accomplish in your life. Try to be brief, because you should memorize your dream statement to the point that you can recite it. By doing this, your dream statement activates the army of helpers in your brain–connecting neu-

                                    MARJORIE BARCOMB

ral pathways to provide insight that you would not have thought of otherwise.

CHARACTERISTICS/ATTRIBUTES YOU WOULD LIKE IN YOUR LIFE

- happy
- good character
- mannerly
- polite
- team player
- well-groomed
- shows initiative
- exercises
- forgiving
- good listener
- dependable
- service oriented
- well-adjusted
- courageous
- healthy
- well-liked
- honest
- fun-loving
- good communicator
- good attitude
- fiscally responsible
- caring
- kind
- accountable
- good relationships
- altruistic
- confident
- persistent
- smart
- cooperative
- loyal
- trustworthy
- responsible
- organized
- exhibits integrity
- critical thinker
- optimistic
- leader/follower
- friends
- moral
- self-controlled
- focused
- wise
- punctual
- reliable
- productive
- respectful
- spiritual
- enjoys leisure time
- loving

- open to ideas
- coping skills
- family oriented
- creative
- social
- committed

Two sample Dream Statements follow:

My primary dream is to become successful and happy so that I may radiate inner beauty by being moral, well-adjusted (mentally, physically and socially), respectful, responsible, financially sound, God loving, critical thinking, service-oriented, and an informed and productive author and citizen in our democratic society.

My primary dream is to work in partnership with church, family, and community to create a positive atmosphere in which I can develop as a healthy, fiscally responsible, creative, motivated, moral person who is productive, dedicated to service, pursuing a career in music, with an appreciation for life, and the courage to stand up for what is right.

Now, write your dream statement on a separate piece of paper. This project may require many drafts, but don't give up; it is your roadmap to success—your master plan. Writing your dream statement will probably become one of the most important documents you have ever written, and learning to live by it will probably become the most important decision you will ever make. Rehearse your dream statement

                                                MARJORIE BARCOMB

daily until it becomes a part of who you are, then re-visit your dream statement annually and amend it, if necessary, as your life changes. A well-written dream statement may last for years without any changes.

Do the attributes you have selected from the list above plus the ones that you have added fit under the umbrella of your dream statement? Again, feel free to keep or to change either of the sample dream statements to fit your perception of who you want to become. You may even want to run your completed dream statement by a friend or another trusted individual for their input or stamp of approval.

After you have completed your dream statement, print it, memorize it, and put it on the refrigerator or another location where you will see it at all times. This will help you to stay on track as you work on becoming successful and happy with whom you are and with whom you are becoming. It is crucial that you read your dream statement several times each day for at least thirty consecutive days. Don't miss a day! If you truly want to change your life, you want this dream statement to elicit automatic decisions and responses from you.

Now that you have your dream statement firmly in place, it's time to start writing your short-term objectives and long-term goals to fulfill your dreams. This is an important step because written goals and objectives are accomplished over seventy percent of the time and unwritten goals and objectives are accomplished from about three to seven percent of the time. Clearly, you must write your goals and objectives if you plan to be successful! I'm always amazed that individuals can get nine or ten times as much done when they have written goals and objectives. The best part is that getting things done seems to be so much easier when you have a plan.

GOALS AND OBJECTIVES

There are various descriptions of goals and objectives, but for the purpose of ease of understanding, this book will call goals those long-term expectations you seek, whereas, objectives are much shorter in term and are stepping stones to goal attainment. Remember, at all times both goals and objectives should fit in your life framework or purpose stated in your dream statement.

Many books have been written about goal-setting; however, just setting and writing your goals and objectives is not enough. You must be forward looking, anticipating road-blocks and challenges. This gives you the ammunition to prepare a strategy to mitigate these events should they unfold. Unfortunately, many people write their goals and objectives, and as soon as they encounter a road-block, they surrender and go back to their old ways of feeling defeated. This shouldn't happen to you because you will learn how to be proactive by choosing appropriate strategies for success.

After reading many self-help books and as a former teacher, I find it interesting that people who are successful in the business world write their goals and objectives and track them; likewise, the few teachers who truly become master teachers also write detailed lesson plans wherein they write their daily objectives for each lesson and track them by asking leading questions and by giving exams. If you are lucky, you may have had one of these teachers in your educational experience. The connection between these two is so clear and simple that I'm surprised that in all my research I have found no one has noticed or written about the connection.

You will find that you do not have to be a rocket scientist to master these skills. Writing objectives to accomplish that which you are passionate about comes easily. The sky is the limit if you choose to reach for your dreams.

Keep in mind that you start out writing your dream statement which leads to your long-term goals, and then you must write your short-term objectives as stepping stones to fulfilling those goals. Even though you will write these three elements in that order, to make the process simpler to understand, I will start by describing the 'how to' of the short-term objectives because they are the building blocks for goal attainment. If I could use the analogy, it is better to read the recipe and learn the ingredients to make a cake rather than to have someone give you a cake and expect you to come up with the ingredients that made it. The objectives are the ingredients and the goal is the cake. I realize that your goal is a cake, not just ingredients. That is why you write your long term goals before your short term objectives. Once you understand the objective writing road-map, it will be much easier for you to write your long-term goals. Also, there is much positive transfer from objective writing to goal writing. The only difference is that the goal subsumes a bunch of objectives.

It would be wonderful if success was easy, but it takes more than wishing for success. Success is simple, but it is not easy. That's why you need a strategic plan—a plan for success! That's where goals and objectives come in.

THE STRATEGIC PLAN FOR WRITING YOUR GOALS AND OBJECTIVES, FACING CHALLENGES AND DEVELOPING A PROACTIVE PLAN

"You must do the thing you think you cannot do."[1]

The primary elements in your strategic plan of goal and objective development include writing your short-term objectives and your long-term goals, developing a strategy for success by determining possible road-blocks and mitigating or eliminating them, listing required materials/resources, setting a time-line to start and to complete your objectives and goals, and evaluating your progress.

WRITING SHORT-TERM OBJECTIVES

The exciting part about writing your objectives using the format described in this book is that you can see the process all the way through to completion on the same page (sometimes on the same line); that is, you can see all the components dealing with that objective at the same time.

Objectives are simply what you want to do or accomplish; therefore, they must begin with an action verb (See Appendix A). Beginning your objective with an action verb is the only way you can assess whether you have completed the objective partially, fully, or not completed it at all.

A few examples of objectives follow: (Notice they all start with an action verb.)

I will…

1. Eat a nutritious breakfast every day.
2. Exercise 4 times per week for forty-five minutes.
3. Read self-help books for thirty minutes daily.
4. Practice my trumpet for forty minutes, five days per week.
5. Attend Bible Study each Wednesday at six o'clock p.m.

By starting your objectives with an action verb, you can quickly assess whether or not these objectives have been met. Did you eat? Did you exercise? Did you read? Did you practice? Did you attend?

If you write your objectives with the knowledge that you will eventually assess yourself on them, you have a much greater chance of accomplishing them. Besides, that army of workers in your brain is paving the way.

DEVELOPING A STRATEGY FOR SUCCESS

Don't ever underestimate the power of setting objectives and writing them down. When you do this, you turn on the many neural pathways that you consciously do not even know exist in your brain. Have you ever noticed when you go to bed confused about a challenge, you frequently wake up in the morning with it all sorted out? And not only that, the solution seems so simple that you wonder why you hadn't thought of it the night before. The same holds true for writing objectives; it's as though you unleash an army of workers that are putting ideas together without you even knowing it. Your brain is a miraculous organ! Let it work for you!

The power of the mind is an amazing thing. You have developed an unbelievable number of neurological pathways through the years, and they are just waiting for you to tap into them. The most remarkable thing is that you don't even realize they are there. It is like going on a trip and taking a scenic highway that you have never traveled before. You may not have traveled on the highway before. But it was there all the time, and you just came up with the objective to travel that highway, and your strategy to get there was to look at a road map, use your GPS, or look up maps and directions on an Internet site. The same is true of your mind—just tap into what you have developed by writing your objectives, and you will be astounded as to the power and focus that is unleashed as you end up on the super-highways you have already developed called neural pathways.

You tap into the gold mine of your mind by setting objectives!

But you follow a plan for success. Let's take a look at two objectives and prepare a strategy for success–keeping in mind potential road-blocks. Learn to be forward looking–just as a teacher is in the classroom if she/he wants *all* the students to be successful. You want to be successful, too; and you can!

Let's look at the first objective: Eat a nutritious breakfast every day.

The following strategy would potentially derail many road-blocks as shown in parentheses.

1. Get up fifteen minutes earlier (road-block: didn't have time)

2. Plan your breakfast menu for the week (road-block: didn't have the right food)

3. Go shopping to make sure you have everything you need for a nutritious breakfast.(road-block: didn't have nutritious food)

4. Set up your dishes and silverware the night before. (road-block: didn't have time)

Let's look at the second objective: Exercise four times per week for forty-five minutes, and then look at the strategy to see if you can find potential road-blocks that have been derailed.

1. E-mail friends and let them know your workout schedule.

2. Ask friends to join you as you get healthy.

3. Prepare your workout clothes and lay them out the night before.

4. Have gym dues automatically deducted from your checking account.

5. Have your water bottle and towel (if necessary) clean and ready to go.

6. If an emergency arises, have time allocated in a fifth day to exercise.

Can you see how the strategy has eliminated or derailed potential road blocks? The key is you want to be successful.

FACING ROAD-BLOCKS

If you have been forward looking in preparing your strategy, you should be able to successfully execute your objective; there is little need to worry about road-blocks because you have already attended to them. Circumventing or eliminating obstacles prior to attempting to do the objective makes life a whole lot easier. That is why the strategy phase of writing objectives is so crucial.

You will unfortunately run into road-blocks that you had not thought of, and will have to deal with them. That's life. Do not get discouraged; most road-blocks can be mitigated, removed, or derailed with thoughtful alternative planning. This may even require changing your objective for a short time; but make sure you substitute another objective that fits into your master plan, one that you can accomplish that will keep you on your path to successfully realize your dreams.

LISTING REQUIRED MATERIALS/ RESOURCES

The first step in setting objectives is to write them down, starting each objective with an action verb. The second step is to write the strategy you plan to follow to make sure your objective is realized. The third step is to write down all the materials and/or resources you will need to complete your objective.

Preparing the materials in advance to complete your objectives may not sound like a big deal, but many objectives have gone by the wayside because of poor planning of materials and/or resources required.

The first objective we looked at was … Eat a nutritious breakfast each day.

What materials are required? It's pretty hard to eat a

nutritious breakfast without food! Also it is pretty hard to eat a nutritious breakfast without nutritious food. This may require a little planning and shopping. Once the food has been purchased and the manner in which to cook the food has been determined, your materials/resources have been taken care of.

What materials would be required in the case of the second objective that we looked at? Exercise four times per week for forty-five minutes. First, you need exercise clothing and shoes, water bottle, towels, and possibly a gym membership or work-out equipment at home. Again, it's impossible to fulfill objectives without the proper resources.

SETTING A TIME-LINE

Another crucial element in objective attainment is writing the date you will start working on the objective and the date you plan to have the objective completed. Again, that wonderful brain of yours takes over, gets you on track, and keeps you on track if it knows when the task must be started and completed. Do you remember how easy it was to cram right before an exam? However, it is not the end of the world if you miss your target date. That does not mean that you give up! You just change the date or make your objective more reasonable. We will talk more about this in the next chapter—creating a successful feedback loop.

Objectives can have any timeline you choose. You may choose to write some daily objectives, weekly objectives, monthly objectives, and/or yearly objectives. When we get into the longer term objectives, I like to call them goals. Some people write daily objectives; I'll call these people the list people. They get a lot done and never seem overwhelmed. Believe it or not, writing daily objectives is a lot easier than it seems, and it gets easier over time. As a matter of fact, many daily objectives are repeated, so if you write your objectives on a computer, they may just require minor adjustments over time.

In the rubric that follows, you can write your objectives, strategy, materials/resources, assessment, and the start and completion dates for each of your objectives. For daily, weekly, and monthly objectives, you may find it easier to just use a D, W, or M, respectively.

Remember, if you do not set a timeline, the objective is not likely to get accomplished. It will just end up in the 'when I get around to it' wish bin in your brain.

Figure 1 Sample Goals and Objectives Worksheet

Obejective	Type	Strategy	Materials/Resources	Assessment	Start	End
Notes: My Assessment						
Notes: My Assessment						

EVALUATING PROGRESS

When should you assess or evaluate your progress on a daily objective? You will either assess your progress at the end of the day or the first thing the next morning. The wisest thing is to assess your daily objectives in the evening and write your objectives for the next day. Guess what master teachers do? Any guess as to why they are so successful?

What does the assessment loop do for you? It helps you to stay on track and to see if any changes in your strategy, materials, or time-line need to be made. It is amazing how painting a room should take a certain amount of time–until you do it. It is okay to re-adjust. It is even okay to decide that a specific objective needs to be scratched. Just don't give up! Also, when you assess your progress, it may lead you to a new objective that you want to get written down right away. How motivational!

When looking at weekly objectives or those with a specific date, it is good to evaluate your progress once each week, and you should set the time to do this. For example, you may schedule your weekly assessment from ten to eleven on Saturday morning. This evaluation helps you to stay on target. It also gives you the opportunity to fine tune your strategy, to determine what works and what doesn't work. In teacher talk, "Monitor and adjust."

If you have several objectives, you might ask yourself whether you have accomplished the high priority objectives. Also, it is a good time to ask yourself how you feel about yourself and your accomplishments for the week. If you are feeling good about yourself, keep up the good work. If you feel that you have not accomplished enough, remember Rome wasn't built in a day, and you didn't get to this point in your life in a day either. It takes time to change your mental programming. But, it is sure worth the effort!

Writing objectives is an ongoing process like eating and sleeping. Once this becomes part of your daily repertoire, you will accomplish so much that you will be shocked. It makes life so much easier, instead of worrying about getting things done, you are getting things done. Not only that, what you accomplish will be leading you to your goals and fulfilling your dreams.

Figure 2 shows a goals and objectives worksheet completed with the two objectives that we talked about previously. Here you can see where you write your objectives, your strategy for successful objective completion, the materials/resources needed, an assessment and the start and completion date. Following you find a place to write notes. This is where you write your results and whether or not modifications have to be made to realize completion of your objective.

Figure 2 Sample Goals and Objectives Worksheet

Obejective	Strategy	Materials/Resources	Assessment	Start	End
Type (Health & Wellness)			Review: Sat 9-10am		
Eat a nutritious breakfast each day	1. Get up 15 minutes earlier 2. Plan weekly breakfast menu 3. Go grocery shopping Sunday afternoon 4. Set up my place seting the evening before	Juice, eggs, bread, Smart balance, cereal, soy milk, coffee, etc.	How many days out of 7 did I have a nutritious breakfast? How can I do better?		
Notes: My Assessment					
Exercise 4 times per week for 45 minutes	1. E-mail friends and let them know my workout schedule 2. Ask friends to join me as I get healthy 3. Prepare my workout clothes and lay them out the night before 4. Have gym dues automatically deducted from my checking account 5. Have my water bottle and towel (if necessary) clean and ready to go 6. If an emergency arises, have time allocated in a 5th day to exercise	Water bottle, gym membership, workout clothes, gym shoes, socks, towel, transportation	How many days did I work out? How do I feel? What have I learned? What would I change, if anything? Can I do better next week?		
Notes: My Assessment					

TYPES OF OBJECTIVES

There are many types of objectives that will help to direct your life toward the fulfillment of your goals. You may find it helpful to use the following types of objectives as a springboard to writing your own. You may want to categorize your objectives into these larger categories, or you may just choose to write all your objectives and prioritize them. At any rate, the partial list that follows may help.

Personal Objectives

- Read thirty minutes each day about core values.
- Have my nails done each week.
- Organize my office and clean my desk.
- Say good things about myself to improve my confidence.
- Spend ten minutes each day giving thanks.
- And many more.

Health and Wellness Objectives

- Eat balanced and nutritious meals to gain, lose, or maintain weight.
- Exercise at least four times per week for forty-five minutes.
- Have annual check-ups.
- Take nutritional supplements daily to augment dietary deficiencies.
- Take prescription drugs only as a last resort.
- Sleep at least eight consecutive hours each night.
- Go to bed at nine-thirty every night.

- Drink at least half of my weight in ounces of water. Ex: 150 pounds—75 ounces of water.
- Eat five or six small meals, or snacks at two-and-a-half to three hour intervals throughout the day.
- Stay out of the sun from ten o'clock a.m. to four o'clock p.m.
- Stay away from smoking, drugs, and alcohol.
- And many more.

Financial Objectives

- Pay off my credit cards.
- Refrain from charging anything.
- Invest wisely for the future–diversify.
- Buy a house.
- Purchase only what is necessary or for investment purposes.
- Save money.
- Prepare a budget.
- Analyze spending and look for possible cuts.
- Clip and use coupons.
- Check Internet for gasoline prices.
- Use a book-keeping program to track my finances.
- And many more.

Career/Educational Objectives

- Register and take classes for training purposes.
- Register and take classes for a skills certificate.
- Register and take classes for a two-year degree: AAS or AA.
- Register and take classes for a bachelor's degree.

- Register and take classes for an advanced degree.
- Take classes for personal enrichment.
- Read and study topics of interest.
- Attend conferences.
- Listen to mentors.
- Find a mentor.
- Study how to use various computer programs and the Internet.
- Prepare a business plan.
- Find five new customers each month.
- Follow up on all customers.
- Thank at least one person each day–in writing.
- Write a book.
- Practice music, dance, sports, etc.
- And many more.

Leisure-Time Objectives

- Visit at least one museum or art gallery each month.
- Attend concerts, operas, and other musical venues at least once every two months.
- Participate in personal sports such a golf at least one each week.
- Travel to a different part of the United States for at least one week each year.
- Travel to a different part of the world for at least one week every three years.
- Vacation with family at least one week each year.
- Go camping with family and friends at least one week each year.
- Read a good book every month.

- Watch less TV–limit to one hour each day.
- And many more.

Service Objectives

- Perform community service for at least four hours each month.
- Volunteer at least 2 hours each month to help children read.
- Study political issues and candidates positions before voting.
- Visit or assist the elderly and handicapped 1 hour each month.
- Serve on school, college, or hospital boards.
- And many more.

Spiritual Objectives

- Attend church or synagogue weekly.
- Attend Bible study every Wednesday night.
- Pray every morning and evening.
- Set ten minutes aside each day to be alone and meditate.
- Listen earnestly to other's spiritual experiences.
- Read the Bible every day.
- And many more.

Family and Relationships Objectives

- Spend four hours per week as family time–no TV or other distractions.
- Listen to what other family members are saying.
- Work together for the good of the family.

- Love and care for my family.
- Support my family financially, emotionally, and spiritually.
- Play games and share stories with my family.
- Act in a manner that is pleasing to my family.
- Speak in a quiet voice unless I or a family member is in danger.
- And many more.

Legacy Objectives

- Write a book.
- Create a foundation.
- Fund a scholarship.
- And many more.

I have just shown you a partial list of possible objectives you may want to incorporate in your plan for success. This is meant to help you get started; it is by no means comprehensive. Each person's objectives will be very different because all human beings are unique. Consequently, your purposes, desires, and passions in this life are different. Notice that the objectives begin with an action verb.

By now you know how to use your objectives worksheet to write and monitor your short term objectives. Normally, you will use this worksheet to write your longer term goals before you begin working on your shorter term objectives because your objectives are the building blocks of your goals, but you need to know what you want the end result to be. Just as in objective development, you will write your longer term goals, develop a strategy for success, determine potential road-blocks, list required materials/resources, set a time-line, and evaluate your progress. After you write your short-term objectives, you may want to go back and amend your long-term goals.

WRITING LONG-TERM GOALS

Writing your long-term goals is similar to writing your objectives, but easier. Your objectives lead to your goals, and you have already synthesized the plan for success to attain your objectives. In an analogy that I mentioned previously, your goal is to have a cake, but you need to put the ingredients together appropriately so that your cake turns out the way you want it to. The step by step process of adding, mixing, and cooking the ingredients are your shorter term objectives leading to your longer term goal of getting a cake. In an effort to accomplish your objectives, you have taken special care to avoid possible pit-falls that you may have encountered each step of the way on your path to your goal attainment. As you continue to refine and amend your objectives, you are finding and reading the right road map to take you on your journey to your goals being fulfilled.

As with your objectives, your goals should start with an action verb. For example … play and win in the World Series. Your strategy is to write and complete your objectives that will lead you to this goal, and you will need to decide on a date for goal attainment. This last step is an unbelievable motivator. It helps you to focus your energies and keeps you on track. It also unconsciously commands the army of helpers in your brain to keep the troops moving. You also need to determine how often you will read and truly reflect on your long-term goals and do a formative evaluation using your objectives to determine how far you have come. You may even want to place benchmark goals at ¼, ½, and ¾ the way to your final goal attainment. You should use the same worksheet for your goals that you use for your objectives. (See Appendix B)

DEVELOPING A STRATEGY FOR SUCCESS

Just as the master teacher must write daily lesson plans, you, too, must write your daily, weekly, monthly, etc. objectives to move you toward your goal. I know you want to be successful otherwise you wouldn't be reading this book. The objectives/goals worksheet I have prepared for you should assist you as you begin your journey to your new life–a happy and successful one.

FACING ROAD-BLOCKS

Your road-blocks should have been mitigated or eliminated as you have modified, amended, deleted, or added to the objectives you have worked on as stepping stones on your way to attain your goal. You know how to do it! You have the plan for success!

LISTING REQUIRED MATERIALS AND RESOURCES

Always have all the materials and resources you need to complete your goals. It is too easy to put off your required action until tomorrow when your required materials are not available. Simply put, be prepared. You certainly wouldn't compete in an Olympic swim competition without being prepared. Your life and your direction are just as important to you as the swim competition is to the contender, and it is dependent on the completion of your goals.

EVALUATING PROGRESS

Just as you assessed your objectives, you will likewise assess whether or not your goals have been accomplished. If your goal has not been accomplished, analyze the steps (the objectives leading to your goal) in your plan. Do you need to move the deadline? Do you need to take courses? Do you need to add some objectives? Do you need to be more dedicated to completing your objectives? How badly do you want this goal fulfilled? If you have the desire and the passion, you will do whatever it takes. You may want to re-read this chapter to get a clearer picture of 'how to' make it to where you want to go. Bless you. I know you are on the right track. Just don't say, "I'll try." Say, "I will."

CREATING A SUCCESSFUL FEEDBACK LOOP

*"I do the very best I know how—the
very best I can; and I mean to keep
doing so until the end ... I walk slowly
but I never walk backward."*[1]

A successful feedback loop is a continuous cycle of monitoring and evaluating objectives, making course corrections or adjusting when necessary, and continuing on to the achievement of an objective—ultimately leading to a worthwhile goal. Once you have met a pre-requisite objective, you are ready to begin your next objective, and so on. It is wise to be working on several objectives simultaneously. If your objectives have not been met to your satisfaction, they may need to be adjusted, amended, or revised depending on the barriers or obstacles you encountered on your journey to their completion. Don't get discouraged; this is a learning process. Again that's life, and it is just part of the process of personal development or personal enrichment that is the conduit to the happiness and success you deserve. Your effort now will make immeasurable improvement in your life over time.

If you plan to become successful establishing goals and objectives and achieving them, you have to be psychologically ready. You must program your brain that you will persevere until you have reached your desired outcome. That means you have to be passionate, driven, and clear about why you want to reach your goals. Many in the self-help industry call this, your "why". If the necessary elements are in place, you have achieved a state of readiness, and you are prepared to launch into your journey. Always write down your start date.

You launch into your journey using a clear, easily executable plan by following the steps set forth in the goals and objectives worksheet. After you fill out your goals and objectives worksheet, tell everyone—tell the world about what you plan to accomplish. This becomes an exceptionally motivational force for you to hang in there when the going gets tough. Remember, Mohammed Ali told the world, "I am the king" and I'm sure that was very motivational for him.

Persistence and perseverance are keys to the realization of your objectives. Program yourself in advance that you will never give up—no matter what. Learn from your mistakes, and get better and better each day at monitoring and adjusting your trip to your final destination of achieving your dreams and aspirations. Let all your mistakes or impediments become valuable lessons in life.

Do you recall the story about the tortoise and the hare? Who wins? It's the one who keeps going, doesn't get sidetracked, stays focused, and keeps his or her eye on the prize. You must bear in mind that the same is true for you. How fast you get there isn't as important as getting there.

The time it takes you to realize your goal or objective depends on the number of and the magnitude of intervening events and your passion or desire to succeed. When you encounter obstacles, you must carefully evaluate your options. What changes must you make to get you to the finish-line? Just as you may have had to adjust, amend, or revise your objectives, you may have to adjust, amend, or revise your strategy, material and/or resources, or your objective completion date. Monitor and adjust! Your journey may take a little longer, but the reward is worth the effort.

Think of the space shuttle astronauts who make continuous course corrections, always keeping their eyes on their destination—the space station. They can't just quit! They can't say, "I don't want to do this anymore. I want to turn around and go home." When you become passionate enough or your "why" is big enough about the accomplishments you desire, you won't be able to quit either; you will keep your eyes on the prize and persevere to the end. Keep in mind that the bigger your goals, the more barriers you will face. Your determination must be like a mighty hurricane!! "Circumstances do not make the man. They merely reveal him to himself."[2] Let the energizer bunny be one of your role models.

In a Nutshell, You Must:

- Have achieved a state of readiness; that is, you must be psychologically ready to begin your journey to goal attainment. Your "why" has to be big enough to give you a sense of urgency.
- Be crystal clear about what your goal is.
- Write your objectives as stepping stones to realizing your goals.

- Think through your strategy to mitigate barriers or road-blocks.
- List the materials and/or resources you will need to complete your objectives.
- Decide on a completion date for your objectives and your goals.
- Be prepared to adjust, amend, or revise your objectives, your strategy, your materials and/or resources, and your completion date. Don't let temporary setbacks discourage you. This does not mean failure!
- Begin your journey by daring to step out of your comfort zone, overcoming fears and doubts. If this is still a problem, you must go back and work on your self-discipline, your self-confidence, and your self-worth.
- Be determined to finish—no matter what. To achieve something you have never achieved before, you must change what you are now doing–you must do something you have never done before.
- Select a time and day to assess your progress. After assessing your progress, make the necessary changes, and repeat the process. If you have completed your objective, go back to the objective worksheet, write the new objective(s) and start the process again.
- Continue doing your self-talk, mental imagery and daily monitoring of your actions.

When you evaluate your progress, make sure to praise yourself even for the smallest improvement. You are at a better place than you were before you started your journey to success and happiness. Be thankful for what you have learned, and the progress you have made. Bear in mind, you are like a freight train; you start out slowly, pick up a head of steam, and exponentially increase your speed toward your destination. This is because you are learning to use a system for success. The more you use the system, the easier it gets.

Share your progress with a friend, family member, or confidant. Explain your successes, trials, and tribulations in your goal attainment process. You will find that as you talk about the steps you have taken, your army of helpers will again be unleashed, and they will help you over, around, or through any obstacle you may have encountered.

"No man is free unless he is the master of himself."[3] God bless you as you step into a new phase of your life.

ACTION VERBS FOR WRITING OBJECTIVES

Curl	Compare
Act	Compose
Analyze	Construct
Apply	Contrast
Appraise	Control variables
Arrange	Convert
Ask	Cook
Assemble	Copy
Assess	Correct
Attend	Create
Bake	Criticize
Blend	Crochet
Boil	Curl
Brake	Cut
Broil	Cut and paste
Brush	Debate
Build	Deduce
Calculate	Defend
Call	Define
Chart	Define
Chop	Demonstrate
Classify	Describe
Clean	Design
Collect	Develop
Color	Diagram
Combine	Dice

Differentiate
Disassemble
Discuss
Display
Dissect
Distinguish
Do
Dramatize
Draw
Draw conclusions
Drill
Drive
Eat
Editorialize
Email
Embroider
Employ
Estimate
Evaluate
Execute
Exercise
Experiment
Explain
Express
Extrapolate
File
Find
Forecast
Formulate
Fry

Gain
Get up
Go
Grade
Graph
Grind
Hypothesize
Identify
Illustrate
Indicate
Infer
Inspect
Interpolate
Interpret
Invent
Investigate
Judge
Knit
Label
Lecture
Light
List
Load
Locate
Look at
Make
Match
Measure
Meditate
Memorize

Mimic	Relate
Mix	Repeat
Nail	Report
Name	Reproduce
Observe	Research
Operate	Review
Organize	Roast
Outline	Role play
Paint	Run
Paste	Sand
Perform	Sauté
Pin	Saw
Plan	Schedule
Play	Score
Practice	Scrub
Predict	Search
Prepare	Select
Present	Send
Print	Separate
Produce	Set up
Program	Sew
Pronounce	Shift
Propose	Shop
Prove	Show
Rate	Simmer
Read	Simplify
Recall	Sketch
Recognize	Slice
Record	Solve
Reduce	State

Steer
Sterilize
Stitch
Study
Summarize
Survey
Synthesize
Talk
Talk out loud
Teach
Tell
Titrate
Transcribe
Translate
Turn
Turn on
Type
Use
Value
Verify
Wash
Weigh
Weld
Wind
Wire
Write

Figure 1 Sample Goals and Objectives Worksheet

Obejective	Strategy	Materials/Resources	Assessment	Start	End
Type					
Notes: My Assessment					
Notes: My Assessment					

Figure 2 Sample Goals and Objectives Worksheet

Obejective	Strategy	Materials/Resources	Assessment	Start	End
Type (Health & Wellness)			Review: Sat 9-10am		
Eat a nutritious breakfast each day	1. Get up 15 minutes earlier 2. Plan weekly breakfast menu 3. Go grocery shopping Sunday afternoon 4. Set up my place seting the evening before	Juice, eggs, bread, Smart balance, cereal, soy milk, coffee, etc.	How many days out of 7 did I have a nutritious breakfast? How can I do better?		
Notes: My Assessment					
Exercise 4 times per week for 45 minutes	1. E-mail friends and let them know my workout schedule 2. Ask friends to join me as I get healthy 3. Prepare my workout clothes and lay them out the night before 4. Have gym dues automatically deducted from my checking account 5. Have my water bottle and towel (if necessary) clean and ready to go 6. If an emergency arises, have time allocated in a 5th day to exercise	Water bottle, gym membership, workout clothes, gym shoes, socks, towel, transportation	How many days did I work out? How do I feel? What have I learned? What would I change, if anything? Can I do better next week?		
Notes: My Assessment					

A LIST OF POSSIBLE SELF-TALK STATEMENTS

Practice daily self-talk sayings to reinforce the values you need to make rational, defensible decisions.

Integrity

- I am honest.
- I always tell the truth.
- I don't exaggerate.
- I am not tricky.
- I don't hide the truth.
- I never take anything that isn't mine.
- I never copy copyrighted material.
- I don't cheat.
- I don't make excuses.
- Excuses are lies.
- I always keep my promises.
- I never promise anything that I cannot fulfill.
- I stop and think before I make promises.
- My word is golden.
- People can depend on me.
- I always do what I say I will do.
- I always say what I mean and I mean what I say.
- I am always on time.
- I am consistent in my behaviors.
- I don't make people worry.
- I can always be trusted.

- I like to work with trustworthy people.
- I want only trustworthy people as my friends.
- It is my moral duty to be trustworthy.

Forgiveness

- I have a forgiving nature.
- I work on forgiveness every day.
- I am not afraid to ask for forgiveness.
- I am not too proud to ask for forgiveness.
- I am strong, therefore, I forgive.
- I want to forgive.
- Forgiveness sets me free.
- True forgiveness eliminates stress.
- True forgiveness eliminates physical ailments.
- True forgiveness eliminates emotional turmoil.

Respect for Self

- I am not easily led.
- I can think for myself.
- I am willing to make changes.
- I care about myself.
- I am a valuable person.
- I enjoy being an ethical person.
- I value my good reputation.
- I am a person of good character.
- I control my anger.
- I control my temper.
- I choose my words thoughtfully.
- I listen intently.
- I listen twice as much as I talk.
- I give praise to someone every day.

- I do not brag about my accomplishments.
- I do not stretch the truth.
- I do not gossip.
- I praise loudly.
- I do not belittle anyone.
- I spread sunshine.
- I smile a lot.
- People like me.
- I am a good person.
- I am worthwhile.
- I pay my bills on time.
- I don't buy anything I can't afford.
- I don't buy on impulse.
- I don't use credit cards.
- I wait until I can pay cash.
- I control my consumption of alcohol.
- I do not drink alcohol.
- I do not drink more than one drink per day.
- I do not smoke.
- I do not do any illegal drugs.
- I only take prescription drugs when it is absolutely necessary.
- I do not gamble.
- I do not over-eat.
- I do not eat junk foods or foods with preservatives.
- I eat a balanced diet.
- I supplement my diet with vitamins and minerals.
- I exercise 4 times per week.
- I do not participate in illicit sexual activity.
- I dress appropriately for the occasion.

- I do not dress like a bum.
- I do not dress like an exhibitionist.
- I control my time.
- I do not waste time.
- I plan ahead.
- I use my calendar.
- I am organized.
- I am confident.
- I go out of my way to eliminate stress.
- I think positive thoughts.
- I detoxify my body.
- I forgive.
- I smile and laugh a lot.
- I sleep at least eight hours each night.
- I drink the required number of ounces of water.
- I am thankful every day.
- I write in my thankfulness journal each day.
- I set goals.
- I read inspirational stories.
- I go to church every…
- I read the Bible every…
- I nurture my spiritual health by…

Respect for Others

- I treat everyone as a gentleman or lady.
- I know everyone has worth in one area or another.
- I always follow the Golden Rule, no matter what.
- I know prejudice and discrimination are disrespectful when it comes to race, religion, stature, intelligence, and other human differences.
- I am tolerant of all that is legal, moral, and good.

                                          MARJORIE BARCOMB

- I am tolerant of cultural differences.
- I respect others' privacy.
- When I call someone, I always ask, "Do you have a minute?"
- I do not call anyone early in the morning or late at night unless it is an emergency.
- I respect others' choice of career.
- I respect others' choice of leisure activities.
- I respect others' choice of relationships.
- I am always courteous and use good manners.
- I do not interrupt others when they are speaking.
- I never take advantage of anyone.
- I listen intently when others are talking.
- I always consider another's point of view.
- I offer constructive information if I think it will help someone.

Respect for Property and the Environment

- I do not waste my time.
- I do not waste natural resources.
- I do not waste my money.
- I respect and maintain my property and possessions.
- I respect the property and possessions of others.
- When I borrow something I always return it clean and in good condition.
- When I rent something from a rental company, I treat it as though it were my own.
- I conserve energy to the best of my ability.
- I never litter our highways or countryside.
- I never pollute our waterways in any way.
- I recycle to the best of my ability.

- I appreciate all that I have and am thankful every day.

Responsibility

- I am not a victim.
- I create my own circumstances.
- I love being busy.
- I am not lazy.
- I take full responsibility for my actions and my life.
- I learn from my mistakes.
- I think out of the box.
- I enjoy being responsible.
- I gain in wisdom every day.
- I appreciate my freedom.
- I think before I act.
- I do not jump to conclusions without all the facts.
- I do not blame others or circumstances for my mistakes.
- I am dependable.
- It is my duty to be loyal to my country in all that is not immoral.
- It is my duty to be loyal to my family in all that is not immoral.
- I obey the laws.
- I pay my fair share of taxes.
- I pay my bills.
- I keep my promises.
- I honor all my contracts both oral and written.
- I am a productive member of society.
- I am loyal to my employer.
- I am always on time.

- I pursue excellence in everything I do.
- I take pride in my work.
- I always go the extra mile.
- I do menial tasks with a good heart.
- I believe in entrepreneurship.
- I nurture and practice my skills and talents.
- I give one hundred percent.
- I do not give up until the job is completed.
- I honor my parents.
- I teach my children the universal standards of civility.
- I treat everyone with respect.
- I listen to the ideas of others.
- I always practice self control.
- My destiny depends on me and me alone.
- I live by the ethical principles laid out in the universal standards of civility.
- My life has a purpose and that is to make this world a better place.

Loyalty and Faithfulness

- I look out for my family.
- I look out for my friends.
- I always keep secrets.
- I never gossip.
- I think before I talk.
- I value my relationships, therefore, I am loyal.
- I am always loyal to my employer.
- I am loyal to my country.
- I study my nation's history.
- I study my nation's founding documents.

- I read about my nation's founding fathers.
- I read, I study and I come to my own conclusions.

Service

- I serve on an in-kind board at…
- I volunteer at the…
- I visit the…
- I read to the…
- I teach…
- I provide transportation for the…
- I pick up trash and keep my neighborhood clean.
- I recycle.
- I dispose of items correctly.
- I participate in the political process.
- I attend meetings that affect my country's future.
- I vote for issues only when I understand them.
- I vote for candidates only when I have studied their voting records.
- I study the issues facing our nation and its future.
- I serve in the military.
- I donate a _____ hours to community service each month.
- I obey all the rules and laws provided they are not immoral.
- I donate money to…
- I donate my expertise to…
- I write a column in the…
- I do spots on the local radio to…

Fairness, Caring and Thankfulness

- I think through all the facets of fairness before I make a decision.
- I take the time to make sure my decisions are fair.
- I help others who are in need.
- I pray for others.
- I am sympathetic when I see hurt or pain.
- I show compassion towards those who have been hurt in any way.
- I am thankful each day.
- I make a list of all the things I am thankful for.
- I read my thankfulness list every day.
- I always lend a helping hand to those who need it.

ENDNOTES

Introduction

[1] Martin Fischer, http://www.wisdom-quotes.com/cat_wisdom.html.

[2] Doc Childre and Deborah Rozman, http://www.wisdomquotes.com/cat_wisdom.html.

Universal Standards Provide You with a Solid Foundation upon which to Build Your Life

[1] Marie Curie, Wisdom Quotes: Quotations to inspire and challenge—by Jone Johnson Lewis http://womenshistory.about.com/od/quotes/a/marie_curie.htm

[2] Lydia M. Child, Think Exist. Capella The University Online, http://thinkexist/quotes.com

[3] Edwin Delattre, Character Counts Seminar, Marina del Rey, CA Nov. 18–21, 1997, *What is Character*, P. 3, Slide 9.

[4] Thomas Lickona, *Educating for Character: How our Schools Can Teach Respect and Responsibility*, A Bantam Book Publishing Co. 1992, P.53

[5] Proverbs 4:23 (NCV) Joe West Photography, http://www.joewestphoto.com/chpobecawhyo.html

[6] Michael Josephson, Character Counts Character Development Seminar, Marina del Rey, CA Nov.18–21, 1997, *Ethics*, P. 4, Slide 12.

[7] Michael Josephson, Character Counts Seminar, *Strategies & Techniques*, P. 31, Slide 92.

8 Michael Josephson, Character Counts semi-
    nar, *What is Character*, P. 3, Slide 7.
9 Theodore Roosevelt, in William J. Bennett
    and Edwin J. Delattre, "Character the Old-
    Fashioned Way," *The Weekly Standard, Vol.
    6, No. 46 [August 20–27, 2001]*, P. 16.
10 J. G. Holland, *Words of Wisdom 4 U,* by Catherine
    Pulsifer editor. http://www.wow4u.com.

Integrity Makes You Morally Whole

1 Michael Josephson, Character Counts
    Seminar, *Trustworthiness*, P. 5, Slide 15
2 George Washington, Brainy Quote, University
    of Notre Dame, http://www.brainyquote.com/
    quotes/authors/g/george_washington.html.
3 Mohammed, *WiseSkills, Princpal
    Notebook:Resources for School Principals*, Legacy
    Learning, 1995, Quotations, P. 34.
4 William Shakespeare, Polonius's last piece of
    advice to his son Laertes in *Hamlet,* Act
    1, Scene 3, E-notes, http://enotes.com/
    Shakespeare-quotes/thine-own-self-true.
5 Shad Helmstetter, *What To Say When You
    Talk To Yourself,* Pocket Books, a Division
    of Simon & Schuster, Inc. 1982
6 Shad Helmstetter, Keynote Speaker, Arbonne
    National Conference, Apr. 2006.
7 William Hazlitt, *Finest Quotes*, Finest Quotes,
    An online community for business women,

http://www.finestquotes.com/author_quotes-
author-William%20Hazlitt-page-0.htm.

8 Jesus Christ

9 King Solomon, WiseSkills Quotes, P. 34

10 Jeff Olson, as quoted by Michael Clouse, Nexera
Empowering the Entrepreneur, *The Purpose of
Commitment,* http://www.nexera.com/mem-
bers/purpose-of-commitment.htm .

11 Dennis Waitley, http://www.quote-
garden.com/promises.html.

12 Ann Fanshawe, Taken from *The Memoirs
of Ann Lady Fanshawe* (1625–1680) c
1670, WiseSkills Quotes P. 34

13 Ninon de Lenclos, WiseSkills Quotes, P. 34

14 David Armistead, http://www.academicintegrity.org/
fundamental_values_project/quotes_on_trust.php.

15 Proverbs 10:9 (AMP)

Forgiveness and Reconciliation Set You Free

1 Alexander Pope, Brainy Quotes, http://brainyquote.
com/quotes/authors/a/alexander_pope_4.html .

2 Catherine Marshall, WiseSkills Quotes, P47

3 Jennifer Thompson-Cannino and Ronald Cotton,
*Picking Cotton: Our Memoir of Injustice and
Redemption,* St. Martin's Press, N. Y. 2009

4 Alexander Pope, Brainy Quotes, http://brainyquote.
com/quotes/authors/a/alexander_pope_4.html .

Respect for Self, Others, and the
Environment Provides for Teamwork, and
Builds Solid Personal Relationships

[1] Confucius, Brainy Quotes, http://www.brainyquotes.com/quotes/authors/c/confucius_4.html

[2] Henry Wadsworth Longfellow, WiseSkills Quotes, P. 21.

[3] Abraham J. Heschel, Jewish Theologian and Philosopher (1907–1972),Think Exist, http://thinkexist.com/quotes/like/self-respect_is_the_fruit_of_discipline-the_sense/6956/

[4] George William Childs, Famous Quotes, http://www.famous- quotes.com/author.php?aid=1491.

[5] Henry Smith Williams, *History of the World,* Quote by Catherine II of Russia, P. 425, http://www.bing.com/search?q=catherine%20II%20Of%20Russia%20quotes&form=HPNTL.

[6] Arabian Proverb, Heart Quotes: Quotes of the Heart. http://heartquotes.net/Hope.html.

[7] Peter J. D'Adamo, *Eat Right 4 Your Type,* Riverhead Books, The Berkley Publishing Group. N. Y. 2002, P. 552.

[8] Brian Tracy, *7 Tips to Boost Your Sales,* http://successnet.czcommunity.com/words-of-wisdom/7-tips-to-boost-your-sales/2750/ May 2009.

[9] Chief Joseph, Brainy Quotes, http://www.brainyquotes.com/quotes/authors/c/chief_joseph_3.html.

[10] Jesse Jackson, Think Exist, http://thinkexist.com/quotes/jesse_Jackson/.

[11] Michael Josephson, Character Counts Seminar, *Respect,* P. 9, Slide 25.

                    MARJORIE BARCOMB

[12] Adolph Hitler, Western Kentucky University, http://wku.edu/teaching/db/quotes/bythinking.php.

[13] Marya Mannes, http://www.stresslesscountry.com/environment-quotes/index.html.

Responsibility Makes You Worthwhile

[1] William Shakespeare, Think Exist, http://thinkexist.com/quotation/we_make_guilty_our_disasters_the_sun_the_moon/263850.html.

[2] Charles Sykes, *A Nation of Victims: The Decay of the American Character*, St Martin's Press, N.Y. 1992.

[3] Anne Frank, About.com: Classic Literature, by Esther Lombardi, http://classiclit.about.com/od/frankanne/a/aa_afrankquote.htm

[4] Hellen Keller, Quotes.net, http://www.quotes.net/quote/5970

[5] Confucius, WiseSkills, P. 27.

[6] Marie Curie, Just Quotes, http://www.justquotes.com/marie_curie_quotes.html

[7] William Jennings Bryant, The Quotations Page, http://www.quotationspage.com/quotes.php3?author=williams+jennings+bryan.

Loyalty and Faithfulness Provide You Love and Security

[1] Marcus Tillius Cicero, WiseSkills Quotes, P. 22

[2] Magic Johnson, WiseSkills Quotes, P. 26.

[3] Aristotle, Brainy Quotes, http://www.brainyquote.com/quotes/authors/a/aristotle_2.html.

[4] Ralph Waldo Emerson, Wisdom Quotes

by Jone Johnson Lewis, http://www.wis-
domquotes.com/cat_friendship.html
5 Mike Shelton, Guest Staff Writer "Lack
of Civic Knowledge is Alarming," *The
Yuma Sun*, April 25, 2009, P. A-4.

Service Provides Intrinsic Rewards and Increases Your Self-worth

1 Eleanor Roosevelt, Quote DB, http://
quotedb.com/quotes/2433.
2 Marian Wright Edelman, Service Quotes
from Wisdom Quotes, http://www.wis-
domquotes.com/cat_service.html

Fairness, Caring, and Thankfulness Earn You Respect

1 Mother Theresa, Think Exist, http://thinkex-
ist.com/quotes/mother_theresa/2.html
2 Thomas Jefferson, Thomas Jefferson was
the principal author of the Declaration of
Independence, http://en.wikipedia.org/wiki/
United_States_Declaration_of_Independence.
3 Saint Paul, WiseSkills, P. 41
4 Faith Baldwin., WiseSkills, P.20
5 J. B. Massieu, Spoken Words: Thanks, http://
www.anand.to/quotes/?keyword=thanks.
6 http://help.com/
post/115969-if-we-reduced-the-world-population.
7 http://help.com/
post/115969-if-we-reduced-the-world-population.

A Decision-Making Model Helps You
Make Defensible, Rational Decisions
with a Clear Conscience

1 Roy Disney, About.com:Quotations, http://quotations.
    about.com/cs/inspirationquotes/a/DecisionMaki5.htm
2 Faith Baldwin, Wisdom Quotes, http://www.
    wisdomquotes.com/033408.html.

On the Surface, Who Do You Think You Are?

1 Martin Buxbaum, Finest Quotes, http://www.
    finestquotes.com/author_quotes-author-
    Martin%20Buxbaum-page-0.htm.
2 Ogden Nash, Quotes and Poems, http://www.famous-
    poetsandpoems.com/poets/ogden_nash/quotes.
3 W. Clement stone, Brainy Quotes, http://
    www.brainyquote.com/quotes/quotes/w/
    wclements392258.html.
4 http://www.jungleswife.com/2009/07/unborn-
    babies-have-short-term-memory.html.
5 http://www.opposingviews.com/i/new-study-says-
    unborn-babies-have-short-term-memory

How Have Your Life Experiences Affected You?

1 Anne Frank, About.com: 20th Century
    History, Anne Frank's diary entry on July
    6, 1944, http://history1900s.about.com/od/
    annefrank/a/AnneFrankQuotes.htm.

Building New Neural Pathways: Replacing
Negative or Destructive Thoughts and
Habits with Positive Constructive Ones

[1] King Solomon, Proverbs 4:23 (NCV).

[2] Rhonda Byrne, *The Secret,* Beyond Words
Publishing, Hillsboro, OR, 2007. et passam.

Perseverance in the Face of Challenge
Facilitates Your Success

[1] Harriet Beecher Stowe, Famous Quotes & Authors,
http://www.famousquotesandauthors.com/
authors/harriet_beecher_stowe_quotes.html.

[2] Calvin Coolidge, The Quotations Page, http://www.
quotatonspage.com/quotes/Calvin_Coolidge/.

[3] Joseph Billings, California State University
East Bay, http://www.edschool.csueastbay.
edu/services/cce/quotes/patient.htm.

[4] Thomas Edison, Great Inspirational Quotes,
http://www.great-inspirational-quotes.
com/persistence-quotes.html.

[5] Author Unknown, http://www.great-inspira-
tional-quotes.com/persistence-quotes.html.

[6] Brian Tracy, *The Power of Persistence,* June
28, 2009, http://www.homebizonline-
success.com/personal-development/
the-power-of-persistence-by-brian-tracy.

[7] Zig Ziglar, SuccessNet Online, *Hold Your Own Feet
to the Fire,* by Brian Tracy, Feb 1, 2009, http://
successnet.czcommunity.com/words_of_wisdom/
hold-your-own-feet-to-the-fire/1590.

　　　　　　　　　　　MARJORIE BARCOMB

[8] Albert Hubbard, ibid.

[9] William Shakespeare, Part 3, Act 2, http://www.william-shakespeare.info/act2-script-text-henry-vi-part3.htm.

The Value of Writing Your Dream Statement and of Setting Goals and Objectives

[1] Joshua Ben Sira, WiseSkills, P. 40.

[2] Queen Christina of Sweden, About Com: Women's History, http://womenshistory.about.com/od/quotes/a/queen_christina.htm.

The Strategy for Writing Your Goals and Objectives, Facing Challenges, and Developing a Proactive Plan

[1] Eleanor Roosevelt, http://wku.edu/teaching/db/quotes/bythinking.php.

Creating a Successful Feedback Loop

[1] Abraham Lincoln, Abraham Lincoln Research Site, *The Inner Life of Abraham Lincoln: Six Months at the White House* by Francis B. Carpenter, University of Nebraska Press, Lincoln, Nebraska, 1955, pp.258–259, http://home.att.net/~rjnorton/Lincoln78.html.

[2] Epictetus, It's All Wrong, Quote:Circumstances, http://allwrong.wordpress.com/category/quote/

[3] Epictetus, http://thinkexist.com/quotes/epictetus/.

listen|imagine|view|experience

AUDIO BOOK DOWNLOAD INCLUDED WITH THIS BOOK!

In your hands you hold a complete digital entertainment package. In addition to the paper version, you receive a free download of the audio version of this book. Simply use the code listed below when visiting our website. Once downloaded to your computer, you can listen to the book through your computer's speakers, burn it to an audio CD or save the file to your portable music device (such as Apple's popular iPod) and listen on the go!

How to get your free audio book digital download:

1. Visit www.tatepublishing.com and click on the e|LIVE logo on the home page.
2. Enter the following coupon code:
   dee4-1220-ccd3-5aed-8d01-9299-5ca5-246a
3. Download the audio book from your e|LIVE digital locker and begin enjoying your new digital entertainment package today!